"It's easy to talk the spi[...] *Spirit*-ual walk? In this boo[...] cal, wise guide to life in the [...] [...] 8. Filled with real-life examples and engaging personal stories, *Walking in the Spirit* is as much a spiritual autobiography as it is an instructional Bible study. Straightforward, humble, and easy-to-read, Berding's book is nevertheless a strikingly deep, important study—the sort of solid spiritual food an increasingly anemic generation should hunger for. *Walking in the Spirit* recalibrates our understanding of the ministry of the Holy Spirit, providing an invaluable corrective to many of us who have either ignored, forgotten, or misunderstood the role of the Spirit in the Christian life."

Brett McCracken,
author, *Hipster Christianity: When Church & Cool Collide*

"At last, a book that I can recommend to the average Christian about holiness, intimacy with God, and the power of the Holy Spirit! In more than twenty years of pastoral ministry I have learned that there is almost universal discouragement—at least at times—in our battle with sin. So many resources offer strategies of accountability or behavior change, but aren't grounded in the deep truth that God *alone* has the power to transform us. Others seem to take a simplistic 'let go, let God' approach that may sound good, but leaves us disheartened when we struggle to live it out. Still others are written at a level that is not readily accessible to all readers. Berding has given us a great gift in *Walking in the Spirit* in that his book is engaging, eminently practical, and most of all, profoundly biblical. If you want to grow deep in your walk with God and experience real power to be like Jesus, you need to read this book."

Robert Bishop, Senior Pastor, Whittier Hills Baptist Church

"Berding captures profound spiritual truths and shares them in a comfortable, down-home fashion that will make you smile, nod, and ponder. When you apply the principles of *Walking in the Spirit*, you will live life differently; you will experience more of the Spirit of God and be able to say with confidence as you approach the end of your life, 'I know Him and am eager to meet Him!'"

Dan LaGasse, missionary, Operation Mobilization

"There is so much confusion among Christians about the Holy Spirit, and I am thankful that Berding has written a much-needed book in layman's language. It is at once biblical, irenic, and charitable. I recommend it to pastors with the hope that they will give copies to their congregations."

Lyle Dorsett, Billy Graham Professor of Evangelism, Beeson Divinity School

"How do I move from a place of *confessing* belief in the Holy Spirit to *experiencing* the Holy Spirit's transforming presence in a more profound way? *Walking in the Spirit* offers us an array of practical insights that will help new believers as well as those who have been Christians for many years."

Clinton E. Arnold, professor and chairman, Department of New Testament, Talbot School of Theology, Biola University; general editor, Zondervan Exegetical Commentary series

"Ken Berding is a man who walks with God in the power of the Spirit. This walk is grounded in Scripture, and through this book we are blessed by the insights of this godly man and first-rate scholar. Those wanting to know more of the Spirit's work in their lives will be helped greatly by what this book offers."

Erik Thoennes, professor of biblical studies and theology, Talbot School of Theology, Biola University; pastor, Grace Evangelical Free Church, La Mirada, California

WALKING
in the
SPIRIT

WALKING
in the
SPIRIT

KENNETH BERDING

WHEATON, ILLINOIS

Trade Paperback ISBN: 978-1-4335-2410-3
PDF ISBN: 978-1-4335-2421-9
Mobipocket ISBN: 978-1-4335-2422-6
ePub ISBN: 978-1-4335-2423-3

Library of Congress Cataloging-in-Publication Data
Berding, Kenneth.
    Walking in the Spirit / Kenneth Berding.
        p. cm.
        Includes bibliographical references (p.   ) and index.
        ISBN 978-1-4335-2410-3 (tp)
        1. Holy Spirit. 2. Christian life. 3. Holy Spirit—Biblical teaching. 4. Christian life—Biblical teaching. 5. Bible. N.T. Romans VIII—Theology. I. Title.
    BT121.3.B47 2011
    234'.13—dc22

                                                            2011010733

Crossway is a publishing ministry of Good News Publishers.

VP   22   21   20   19   18   17   16   15   14   13   12   11
14   13   12   11   10   9   8   7   6   5   4   3   2   1

CONTENTS

PREFACE

═══

his book is an invitation to a journey and a road map to lead you along it. I invite you to join me on an expedition into what the Bible teaches about life in the Holy Spirit. Precious few in our generation seem willing to travel this path. They are too distracted by the cares of life and the noise of our age to even know that something is missing! Won't you come along with me on this journey? My prayer as we travel through this study together is that God will profoundly transform your thinking and reform your affections so that you become passionate about the things of the Spirit and knowledgeable about how to live a life directed by him. Our tour guide is the apostle Paul, a man who had been miraculously set free by the Spirit. Our outline is taken from his words about the Holy Spirit in Romans 8. Romans 8 is sacred ground for Christians who want to walk the *Spirit*-ual walk. We may have to spiritually take off our sandals at the beginning of the journey and bow our hearts before a sovereign Lord who gave us his travel guide and his Spirit to lead us forward.

Some things will be useful for you to know about Romans 8 that are not discussed in the following seven chapters. The reason they are not included is that my goal is to help you learn how to walk in the Spirit; it isn't to write a commentary on Romans 8. Therefore there is an appendix at the back of the book entitled "Three Undercurrents in Romans 8." You can choose to read that section before you begin reading about life in the Spirit, or you can read it later. The appendix lays out three things that you should keep in mind if (and hopefully when) you decide to embark on a deeper study of Romans 8 for yourself.

This book doesn't discuss spiritual gifts. It is unfortunate that the topic of spiritual gifts has overtaken discussions about the Holy Spirit in the past couple of generations. Classes on the Holy Spirit often are dominated by discussions of spiritual gifts. The gravitational center of Paul's teaching about the Holy Spirit is not the so-called spiritual gifts; the center is the constellation of ideas discussed in the pages ahead that is best summarized as *walking in the Spirit*. Because I have already written a book in which I present a biblical challenge to the conventional view of spiritual gifts that is so popular right now among both charismatics and noncharismatics, and because the topic does not play a part in Romans 8, I have chosen to ignore it completely in this book.[1] I expect that both noncharismatics and charismatics will discover help in their journeys in the Holy Spirit as a result of what they read in the pages ahead.

This book is somewhat autobiographical. When I started writing, I determined that I should provide a window into my own spiritual journey related to the work of the Holy Spirit to help you know how to apply what is found in the Bible. So I have peppered these pages with real-life examples. This doesn't mean that I have fully experienced the depths of the ministry of the Holy Spirit in my own life! I sometimes feel that I have barely understood it at all. But from one traveler to another, I want to encourage you in your own journey with the Holy Spirit by looking through the window into my own walk.

In appendix 2 you will find a creative and fun way to *remember* what you have learned. It will help you memorize the seven main points of this book so they can be a constant reminder of how to step out in the Spirit. It is also a creative way to teach this material if you are a teacher.

I want to thank a few people for their help on this book. Robert and Davette Bishop read earlier drafts and offered many helpful bits of encouragement and critique. My father, Drew Berding, once again has lent his keen editing skills to help me think and communicate more clearly. My colleague, Jon Lunde, often dialogued with me both about exegetical issues and about practical aspects of life in the Spirit. Special thanks are due the women of the Entirely His Bible studies at Whittier Hills Baptist Church who read an earlier draft during their Christmas break from studying through the book of Romans. I also want to thank the students from two semesters of my Biblical Interpretation & Spiritual Formation class at Biola University, who were required to read earlier drafts as a class assignment. I so appreciate the deans at Talbot School of Theology, Dennis Dirks and Mike Wilkins, who granted me a sabbatical leave, during which I was able to devote time to this project along with a couple other projects. I am deeply grateful to all the editors and staff at Crossway who caught the vision for a book on walking in the Holy Spirit that was rooted in Romans 8. They have so graciously and expertly shepherded this book all the way from acquisition to distribution. Finally, and especially, I want to thank my wife and life partner, Trudi. We celebrated our twenty-fifth wedding anniversary at the scheduled date for this book's release. She has been my traveling companion during most of the experiences I have shared with you. It is to Trudi that I dedicate this book with joyful gratitude for the incredible gift she has been to me.

I often write music for times of personal prayer and occasionally share them with others when I lead worship. I would like to share the lyrics of one of my songs for you to use as a prayer for receptivity to what the Holy Spirit may want to do in you as you read the pages ahead. Read the song aloud and pray in your heart the words to the Lord.

Spirit of the Living Lord
Softer than a gentle wind, ushering your mercy in
Meet me here . . . Spirit of the Lord
Purer than a burning fire, be my sanctifier
Draw me near . . . Spirit of the Lord
Holy Comforter, gentle breezes blow
Cleansing stream . . . come, my soul restore
Holy fire burn, shining light shine bright
Rushing wind . . . Spirit of the Living Lord
Cleaner than a rushing stream,
ev'ry wayward thought redeem
River flow . . . Spirit of the Lord
Holy Spirit pure and bright,

light the way with holy light,
Jesus show . . . Spirit of the Lord
Holy Comforter, gentle breezes blow
Cleansing stream . . . come, my soul restore
Holy fire burn, shining light shine bright
Rushing wind . . . Spirit of the Living Lord

WALK IN THE SPIRIT

walk a lot. Compared to most people in Southern California I walk *a lot.* My "commute" to work is a fifteen-minute walk. I teach at a medium-sized university where classes are scheduled in rooms all over campus—five to ten minutes *to* class, five to ten minutes *from* class—for every period I teach. I love to take walks with my wife and daughters in the evenings. And for prayer, I know of no better way to pray than by prayer-walking. Others kneel, sit, raise their hands, or journal their prayers. I walk. Walking keeps me awake. It keeps me focused. And it reminds me of something that is profoundly biblical.

I have walked the streets of the great cities in which I have lived over the years: in my home town in California's Bay Area, in the Great Northwest where I went to college, and in Berlin just before the dismantling of the Berlin wall. I walked during the seven years my wife Trudi and I lived in two different Middle Eastern cities. I walked in Philadelphia and in a suburb of New York City while my family lived on the East Coast during my doctoral studies and early years of teaching. And I walk in the place that God has put me now—in the Los Angeles area of Southern California. Walking is one thing I do habitually in my physical life. And it is foundational for my spiritual life as well.

Life in the Spirit is a journey. It isn't sitting in a comfortable deck chair on the veranda of a cruise ship. Neither is it a sprint toward a finish line you can see just ahead. Granted, your journey in the Spirit will sometimes include periods of sitting, and sometimes you will have to sprint. And there are many other good analogies for Christian living. But for the apostle Paul, life in the Spirit is best compared to walking. He launches into his discussion of the ministry of the Holy Spirit with the words at the end of Romans 8:1–4:

> There is therefore now no condemnation for those who are in Christ Jesus. For the law of the Spirit of life has set you free in Christ Jesus from the law of sin and death. For God has done what the law, weakened by the flesh, could not do. By sending his own Son in the likeness of sinful flesh and for sin, he condemned sin in the flesh, in order that the righteous requirement of the law might be fulfilled in us, *who walk not according to the flesh but according to the Spirit.*

Learning to Walk according to the Spirit
If you want to be someone who brings glory to God (and I pray that there is nothing you desire more!), you must

learn what it means to *walk* according to the Spirit. There are no shortcuts on this journey; the only way from here to there is to walk.

In appendix 1 I discuss how Romans 8 is not just about you and me, though it is certainly about that. Paul's discussion about walking according to the Spirit in Romans 8 is part of a larger theme in which Paul contrasts life *then* with life *now*. The *then* was the period dominated by the Law, the period before Christ's death, resurrection, ascension, and sending of the Holy Spirit. But even *then*, the prophets longed for a new age when the Spirit would not simply come upon certain individuals to empower them in special instances. They anticipated and predicted an age when the consummate cleansing for sin would take place and where *walking* in God's statutes would result from the presence of God's indwelling Spirit in all his people. Here is one example of what the Old Testament prophets hoped and longed for:

> I will sprinkle clean water on you, and you shall be clean from all your uncleannesses, and from all your idols I will cleanse you. And I will give you a new heart, and a new spirit I will put within you. And I will remove the heart of stone from your flesh and give you a heart of flesh. And I will *put my Spirit* within you, and *cause you to walk* in my statutes and be careful to obey my rules. (Ezek. 36:25–27)

Ezekiel and the other prophets looked ahead to the day when God would put his Spirit within us. Paul said that this day is now! Paul declared that the requirements of the Law are already fulfilled in us who do not walk according to the flesh but according to the Spirit. That is, the requirements of the Law have been fully taken care of by the death of Jesus Christ on our behalf so that we don't have to live in dependence upon the Law to move us forward in our spiritual lives. Instead, we depend on the Spirit; we walk in the Spirit.

Walking is the apostle Paul's favorite metaphor for the Christian life. That's probably because Paul walked *a lot*. He walked a lot even compared to me! I don't mean that he walked a mile each day for exercise or that he took the stairs instead of the elevator. It has been estimated that Paul traveled around twelve thousand miles during his known missionary journeys, much of it on foot![1] Perhaps that's why he was always comparing our Christian lives to walking. He uses the word we sometimes translate "walk" thirty-two times in his letters! Here are a few examples:[2]

> I therefore, a prisoner for the Lord, urge you to *walk* in a manner worthy of the calling to which you have been called. (Eph. 4:1)

> *Walk* in love, as Christ loved us. . . . (Eph. 5:2)

> We *walk* by faith, not by sight. (2 Cor. 5:7)

> *Walk* by the Spirit, and you will not gratify the desires of the flesh. (Gal. 5:16)

> If we live by the Spirit, by the Spirit let us also *walk*. (Gal. 5:25, NASB)

I like the way the ESV translates this last verse: "If we live by the Spirit, let us also keep in step with the Spirit."

This rendering makes me smile a bit as I think of evening walks with Trudi. There are few things I like to do better than to walk around the neighborhood with her in the cool of the evening to talk about what is going on in our lives and to dream about the future.

And as we walk I sometimes slip my arm around Trudi's waist. The only problem is that if we aren't in step with each other, our hips keep bumping against each other! There's nothing romantic about that. So in order to stop our hips from bumping, we have to get in step with each other. Only then can we enjoy the walk we set out to take.

There is no shortcut to learning how to keep in step with the Spirit—how to walk in the Spirit. The *Spirit*-ual walk is not just for ultraspiritual people. And it isn't the property of charismatic Christians. Walking in the Spirit is the central metaphor for describing what it means to live as a Christian. Life lived according to the Spirit is not simply trying to do the right thing. Nor is it simply trying to live according to God's Law. Life as a Christian is cooperating with the Holy Spirit in a daily walk. The person who walks according to the Spirit will in fact have the essence of the Law fulfilled in his life. God has once and for all "condemned sin in the flesh" through the atoning sacrifice of Jesus, and we have received that gift by faith. The result is that the believer in Jesus Christ is now *free* to live according to the Spirit. He is no longer obligated to live according to the flesh. He will become increasingly dependent upon the Holy Spirit, and any space given to things that displease God will decrease with every passing day.

I know that learning the *walking* side of the Christian life has been enormously important for my own growth as a man who wants to please the Lord more than anything else in life. It won't surprise you that after God really got a hold of my heart as a young man, I was not always in tune with the idea of the Christian life as a Spirit-empowered journey. I was intensely interested in dealing with the *immediate* desire to reach friends with the good news and to waste no time challenging my Christian friends to live radically committed lives to Christ *today*. I longed to see my prayers answered *soon*, and felt keenly the pressing need to overcome sin *in this moment*. But I hadn't yet learned the *Spirit*-ual walk that addresses both the concerns of this moment *and* the long walk of months and years of a faithful and loving relationship with the Lord.

"Walking according to the Spirit" is Paul's shorthand description for all the other things he says about the Spirit in Romans 8. What are the kinds of things you do when you walk in the Spirit?

- You set your mind on the things of the Spirit (v. 5–7)
- You put to death the deeds of the body by the Spirit (v. 13)
- You are led by the Spirit (v. 14)
- You know the Fatherhood of God by the Spirit (vv. 15–17)
- You hope in the Spirit (vv. 23–25)
- You pray in the Spirit (vv. 26–27)

Since walking in the Spirit seems to be an all-encompassing metaphor for Christian living, it also probably includes ideas that are found in other places in Paul's writings, such as being filled with the Spirit (Eph. 5:18), serving in the Spirit (Rom. 7:6; 15:16), and loving by the Spirit (Rom. 15:30; Gal. 5:22–23; Col. 1:8). The *Spirit*-ual walk should include all of these and more.

Pictures of a *Spirit*-ual Walk

But why does Paul have to use so many metaphors and analogies in Romans 8 to describe the Spirit's activities and our relationship to them? Why doesn't he just tell us directly what he wants us to know?

There are many things that are *real* about the Christian life that cannot be reduced to propositional language. This isn't the case for only spiritual realities—though the difficulty is often felt there more acutely than anywhere else; it is also true for many issues in life. For example, how would you describe in concrete words the love a husband feels for his wife or the trust a child has in her mother? I'm not asking how you can tell whether a husband loves his wife or a child trusts her mother. That's easy. You can see love or trust worked out in what they do; the husband does specific loving actions toward his wife, such as spending time talking with her over a cup of tea, and a child demonstrates trust by listening to the advice of her mother. The more difficult question is how to describe what the husband's love *feels* like, or what the child *experiences* when she trusts her mother. Nonmetaphorical language lets you down at that point.

This is why poets and songwriters (and lovers who are neither poets nor songwriters!) use metaphors to express their love. Although imagery cannot communicate all that is there, in certain situations it often communicates more fully than concrete words do. Some things are difficult to communicate with straightforward words. Metaphors *suggest* to our inner selves something that is true about a deeper reality. They also often touch us in our emotions, something direct language often doesn't accomplish as well. This is important, because the passages of Scripture that teach us how to walk *Spirit*-ually should impact our hearts and emotions as well as our actions.

That's why God sometimes chose to use metaphors to describe his own Spirit—wind, fire, rivers of living water— and also to use metaphors to describe things we need to know about our relationship to that Spirit—walking, putting to death, being led, getting adopted, and so forth. This also means, though, that some things we need to learn about walking in the Spirit will only become clear to us as we actually do the walking. You may not know how to describe what it feels like to be led by the Spirit, but if you have walked with the Lord for a while, you may actually know how to follow when you are led.

In light of this, perhaps one way of describing the walk in the Spirit is to imagine what a day would look like if you were walking according to the Spirit.

Your alarm goes off, and the first thing you pray is, "Lord, I want to walk with you during this day." You pull your tired body off of the mattress with the prayer, "I need your help even to get going today." Your first spiritual action of the day is to tangibly express love to each member of your family using a hug, a touch, or a word of genuine care. You spend some time meditating on a section of Scripture and take a walk (or sit or kneel) for prayer where you cry out to God for his grace in the day ahead. You get into your car with the awareness that one of your weaknesses is the way you respond to bad drivers, but before your mind gets carried away you breathe a prayer for God's grace to give you patience on the road. You forgive your boss (teacher, colleague, coworker, brother) with the help of the Spirit as that so-very-difficult person once again says you-know-what to you. You suppress a word of gossip that is trying to creep from your heart toward your mouth and turn your eyes away from something you shouldn't gaze upon. At some point during the day, you express a spontaneous moment of thanksgiving to God for the presence of his Spirit within you. During your drive home, you think about concrete ways you can serve your family, and you ask the Spirit to fill you with strength to live out your convictions even at the end of a long day. You end your day with thankfulness for the Spirit's sustaining grace throughout the day that has just passed.

I've heard it said that a person's character is the sum total of a lot of little choices. Similarly, the *Spirit*-ual walk is the sum total of a lot of little steps taken in submission to God's Holy Spirit.

In the next two chapters I will discuss how we deal with sin and overcome temptation (preview: by setting your mind on the things of the Spirit and by putting to death the deeds of the body by the Spirit). For now, let me just state that as you daily walk in the Holy Spirit, God will fill you with his Spirit in such a way that your desire to sin lessens. Galatians 5:16—which is set in a chapter that parallels Romans 8 in many ways—says it so well:

"Walk by the Spirit, and you will not gratify the desires of the flesh." The one who walks in the Spirit *will not* give in to the desires of the flesh. Walking in the Spirit and carrying out the desires of the flesh are mutually exclusive ideas; you cannot do one at the same time as you engage in the other.

A few years ago Trudi and I went to San Diego for a couple days to celebrate a special birthday. The day we arrived, we dropped off our bags at a hotel and went out to look in some shops. As we walked, we came across one of those ice cream shops . . . you know, the kind that sells waffle cones filled above the brim with creamy, chunky, yummy ice cream. I turned to Trudi and said, "We're on vacation, honey, we can have one of these if we really want." We both agreed that we really *did* want one—each!—but would enjoy it even more the following day since we were heading to dinner soon.

The next day we walked by another one of those amazing ice cream shops selling the same kind of creamy, chunky, yummy ice cream in a waffle cone. I turned to Trudi to pose a question I already knew the answer to: "Now do you want an ice cream?" Her response: "Oh no! That sounds awful. I couldn't possibly eat one of those right now!"

Why not? What could possibly have changed? How could it be that she (and I) craved one of those waffle cone ice creams the previous day, but we didn't want it now? The answer is simple: we were *full*. Actually, we were stuffed. The hotel at which we were staying provided a brunch—a beautiful, extravagant brunch. We had eaten crepes and omelets and waffles and fruit and muffins—far too much of it all. An hour later, when we walked by that incredible ice cream shop, we simply weren't interested anymore. We weren't enticed by the ice cream because we were full of something else.

As you walk in the Spirit, depending upon the Spirit and being filled with the Spirit, your desire to sin will minimize. There is more to say about overcoming sin, but it isn't much more complicated than that. Walk in the Spirit and you will not carry out the desire of the flesh. Be so full of the Spirit that your craving to sin lessens. You won't have the same desire to sin because your walk is along a different path, the way of the Spirit. You'll be moving in a different direction.

Have you learned to walk according to the Spirit?

Last year, perhaps because of all the physical walking I do, my Achilles tendon began to hurt. At first I didn't know that it was my Achilles tendon; all I knew was that the back of my ankle sometimes was sore and a bit swollen after walking. And like most men I know, I waited for five months before going to the doctor, thinking that my problem would go away. The doctor wasn't impressed by my tough-guy act. He warned me that I was on the verge of rupturing my tendon if I didn't take care of it immediately. He put me in a walking boot that immobilized my ankle and raised my heel four inches from the ground. I don't know why they call it a "walking" boot . . . walking is the one thing that cannot be easily done in it. (I will never joke about high heeled shoes again!)

I had to wear that "boot" for seven months! Even at this writing, although I do not have to wear the boot anymore, my ankle is not entirely healed. I can only walk short distances without the pain returning. It has been a more significant challenge to my spiritual life than you may imagine. Please understand, I have been prayer-walking for twenty-five years, and I use my times of daily prayer to bring my heart in line with what God would want me to think about, to prepare for whatever ministry I might have for the day ahead, and for intercessory prayer on behalf of others.

So I have had to learn other postures for prayer, most particularly sitting either in a lawn chair in my little Californian backyard or in a chair in my living room when it is too "cold" to sit outside. God has shown lots of grace to me during this period in which he apparently in his inscrutable wisdom didn't want me to physically walk. I have had to learn to keep walking *Spirit*-ually even when my favorite mode of prayer hasn't been possible.

I have also been reminded during this period of inactivity of the risks of not Spirit-walking on a daily basis. Those who don't walk in the Spirit on a moment-by-moment basis will not be thinking on the things of the Spirit and orienting their minds toward the things that the Spirit desires. Those whose walk is not according to the Spirit will feel the pull of temptation more intensely than those who do. Those who fail to learn to walk in the Spirit never really learn how to be sensitive to the Spirit's promptings. The *Spirit*-ual walk is the foundation for understanding one's identity as a child of the Father. The walk in the Spirit allows one to hope in the midst of suffering. And the *Spirit*-ual walk sets the tone for having a heart lifted up in prayer throughout each day.

Physical therapy has reminded me that it takes time to build up strength and healthy patterns that contribute to long-term walking. My ankle muscles weakened during the time I was wearing the walking boot. I now exercise those muscles every day. Since injuries to the Achilles tendon heal so slowly, I'm reminded that I need to put in place patterns that will allow me to walk next year, and the next, and the next. This is all true about the "walk" that constitutes our spiritual lives as well.

How are your spiritual ankle muscles? Have they atrophied due to inactivity? It will take time to get accustomed to a moment-by-moment, day-by-day walk in the Spirit if this is not the regular pattern of your life. But is this not what you most deeply desire? Can you hear the Spirit calling you to journey with him? My prayer and hope for you is that you will respond to the Spirit's invitation to live a life of dependence and hope and wisdom and courage and holiness and prayer . . . all empowered by the Holy Spirit of God.

So, how do you live life in the Spirit?

1. Walk in the Spirit.

Questions for Review

1. How is life in the Spirit like a journey? Why do you think Paul often compared the Christian life to walking?
2. Did believers during the Old Covenant age (Old Testament age) experience the Holy Spirit in the same way we do now that the New Covenant has begun?

3. Why does Paul use so many metaphors and analogies to describe life in the Spirit?
4. How does walking in the Spirit help us deal with the temptation to sin? (There will be more on this in the next two chapters.)
5. What are some of the risks of not learning how to walk *Spirit*-ually?
6. Do you feel comfortable talking about the Holy Spirit? Why or why not?

SET YOUR MIND ON THE THINGS OF THE SPIRIT

ave you ever had a song stuck in your head? I remember once visiting Disneyland (just down the road from where I live). After the visit I could not get the chorus of the ride "It's a Small World" out of my mind. "It's a Small World (after All)" plays in the background for the entire hour you wait in line, and seems to increase in volume throughout the ten minutes you're on the ride. No matter how hard I tried, for weeks I couldn't get that song out of my head.

Or maybe during your childhood—or your children's childhood—you were inflicted with "The Song That Doesn't End." This infinitely recursive children's song was sung at the close of every episode of the television show *Lamb Chop's Play-Along*, hosted by Shari Lewis. This aggravating song simply doesn't end—ever! It "goes on and on, my friend." (And on, and on, and on . . .)

But the wickedest of all such songs is "The Song That Gets on Everybody's Nerves."

> I know a song that gets on everybody's nerves,
> everybody's nerves, everybody's nerves.
> I know a song that gets on everybody's nerves,
> And this is how it goes . . . (repeat and never stop).

Do you know that song? If you do, go ahead and sing it a few times.

Now try to get it out of your head.

The apostle Paul often writes about something he calls the "flesh." In some ways the "flesh" is a lot like "The Song That Gets on Everybody's Nerves." It plays incessantly in the background and exerts a powerful pull on you. But Paul also reminds us that "those who live according to the Spirit set their minds on the things of the Spirit."

Look at Romans 8:5–8:

> For those who live according to the flesh set their minds on the things of the flesh, but those who live according to the Spirit set their minds on the things of the Spirit. For to set the mind on the flesh is death, but to set the mind on the Spirit is life and peace. For the mind that is set on the flesh is hostile to God, for it does not submit to God's law; indeed, it cannot. Those who are in the flesh cannot please God.

Life in the Spirit has a lot to do with your mind-set. Whatever your *mind* is *set* upon will determine to a large degree how you are doing in your Christian life. If your mind is set on the things of the Spirit, you will indeed discover life, a life characterized by peace. If your mind is set on the flesh, you will experience hostility toward God, you will not be in subjection to the law of God (since you can't), and you will not please God.

A Mind Set on the Flesh vs. a Mind Set on the Spirit

The word translated *mind* or *mind-set* concerns more, however, than just your thinking processes, even if that is a significant part of it. In addition to what you think about, the word also probably refers to what you *desire* and the way your life is directed toward what you desire. This is why I sometimes use the word *mind-set*. I'm talking about the overall orientation of your life—including what you think about—and whether your thoughts and desires are directed toward the things of the Spirit, or whether they are directed toward the flesh.

At age fourteen, God got a hold of my teenaged heart as I began to think about the length of eternity and the brevity of life. Thoughts of eternity became lodged in my mind to such a degree that I simply couldn't keep living the way many of my friends were living. My desire to be used of God to introduce others to Jesus Christ and to be an instrument for bringing revival to his church was growing exponentially. And my life *was* different from most of those around me. The things I longed for and, for the most part, the things I thought about were quite different from what most of my high school friends thought and cared about. I organized prayer meetings, set up outreach days, soaked up the Word of God like a sponge, and prayed

31

my heart out for my friends. Growth was real, and I truly cared to live a life out of step with the world and in step with Jesus Christ.

But there was a problem. Despite how deeply I cared about the things of God, I was desperately aware of how weak I was in certain areas of temptation. I begged God to take away my desires. I fasted and prayed. I memorized Scripture. I set up systems of accountability with my friends. But it was war. Like the song that gets on everybody's nerves, temptations seemed relentless. And worst of all, when I actually did something or allowed myself to think about something that didn't please the Lord, the sensation was dreadful, like I had abandoned the Lord. I was a sincere and passionate Christian teenager struggling with the clash between the mind-set of the Spirit and the mind-set of the flesh.

So what do we do about the pull of the flesh? First we need to answer the question, what is the flesh?

The problem with answering this question is that there is no single English word that works well to translate the Greek word we're interested in (*sarx*). Some translations just use the word *flesh* and hope that a teacher somewhere will explain what it means. The difficulty of course, is that when we use the English word *flesh*, we tend to think about *meat* or physical *bodies*, and that is not what Paul is writing about in this passage and many others like it. Less literal translations try to explain the expression, using something more easily understood. The most common attempt is the expression *sinful nature*. But there is a serious problem with such a translation since it introduces an idea that isn't there. The translation *sinful nature* implies that there are two parts of a person's inner self—a spiritual nature and a sinful nature. But I don't think that is what Paul wanted to communicate. This passage—and others like it in Paul's writings—was not written to explain the make-up of a person's immaterial self; its focus is upon one's tendencies, thoughts, impulses, and desires.

The *flesh* in Romans 8:5–8 is the tendency that everyone feels to be pulled back into sin. It is the inclination to sin that everyone who lives in a body experiences that must be overcome by the Holy Spirit. It is the weakness I was so frustrated about as a Christian young man. Think of it as the gravitational pull toward sin. As with gravity, everyone feels its force. It's the downward pull that everyone faces who is a descendent of Adam (Rom. 5:12–21) and who has the habit of sinning. (Are you in that category? Yes. Paul says that everyone is.)

But that doesn't mean you're stuck on the ground if you truly know Christ! So how is the power of the flesh overcome? The first—and foundational—way Paul mentions in Romans 8 is having your mind set on the things of the Spirit. Even as a teenager, I began to notice that when my mind was filled with the things of God, the desires to sin would lessen. This is because thinking on the things of the Spirit is like getting into a hot air balloon. Gravity—our analogy for the pull of the flesh—is still there, and you had better be aware of its power, but the person living in the Spirit is no longer stuck on the ground. The gravitational pull of the flesh has no power over the one whose mind is set on the things of the Spirit.

Leon Morris describes those who have this Spirit-oriented mind-set: "Such people are not intermittently interested in the things of the Spirit; their whole being centers on them. What the Spirit does is their absorbing interest.... It is a delighted contemplation of what the Spirit does wherever the Spirit chooses to move."[1]

During my last two years of high school I was a student in a speech and drama elective class. My teacher devised an interesting activity to teach us how to stay in character when acting. We were assigned a passage of a play to memorize and then called up to recite it in character at the front of the class. But what made this activity particularly fun and challenging was that the other students were invited to do whatever they could to distract the speaker from staying in character.

I remember how difficult it was to stay in character while the guy in the front row was putting his fingers in his nose or someone over on the left side of the room was making unpleasant sounds that caused everyone to laugh uncontrollably. It required "thoroughgoing concentration"—an expression Morris uses to describe the mind set on the Spirit—to keep in character.[2] But when it was my turn to stand before this raucous crowd, I focused on a point in the back of the room, concentrated on my monologue, and successfully kept in character despite the interference. So just as I resisted the distractions in the audience by focusing on that one point, the way to overcome the pull of the flesh is by focusing on the things of the Spirit.

A Spirit-Oriented Mind-Set

But there is a problem with my analogy. It implies that thinking on the things of the Spirit is just focusing on God during a period of temptation. I tried really hard to stay in character in my drama class, so much so that I would sometimes bite my tongue or cheek for a moment so that the pain would counteract the desire to laugh! (I remember biting my tongue hard enough one time that it started to bleed.) But the mind set on the Spirit is not just about what you do in the moment of temptation. It is a reorienting of your thoughts, your desires, and your motivations, so that a Spirit-oriented focus becomes the established pattern of your life.

It might be helpful to imagine your thoughts as scheming inmates who are plotting a jailbreak. (The tendency of your thoughts to jailbreak is one aspect of the flesh.) Your thoughts need to be trained so that they stay on the things the Spirit produces, such as love, joy, peace, patience, kindness, goodness, faithfulness, gentleness, and self-control (Gal. 5:22–23). Normally, your thoughts will try to escape toward jealousy, envy, anger, sensuality, immorality, and even idolatry (Gal. 5:19–21). But you have been called, as Paul says in 2 Corinthians 10:5, to "take every thought captive to obey Christ."

In daily life this means that you talk to God throughout the day. You fill your mind with songs of worship and you keep directing them upward. You let your thoughts *dwell* on things that are true, honorable, just, pure, lovely, commendable, excellent, and praiseworthy (Phil. 4:8). You actively, by the Spirit, reject wrong thoughts as they come in.

Sometimes as I'm walking, a thought will pass through my mind that I know doesn't please the Lord. I'll immediately and suddenly say "stop it!" to that thought. (Sometimes the "stop it!" comes out really loud, and I find myself looking around to see if anybody has heard me!) In other words, I rebuke whatever thoughts are not pleasing to the

Lord and redirect my thoughts so that they are once again captive to the obedience of Christ.

One of the best things about growing older is that redirecting my thoughts is a lot easier to do now than it was when I was younger. Notice that I didn't say it was automatic. As I will discuss in the next chapter, spiritual passivity is not the way to move forward in a life of holiness. But I do find after many years of thinking on the Spirit that a mind directed toward the Spirit has become the regular orientation of my life.

Unfortunately this isn't the case for many who are my age and older. Some people have day after day, month after month, year after year filled their minds with drivel rather than with the things of the Spirit. *Dictionary.com* defines *drivel* as either "saliva flowing from the mouth" or "childish, silly, or meaningless talk or thinking." Rather than filling their hearts and minds with the things of the Spirit, most people in this entertainment-saturated generation—even professing Christians—fill their minds with meaningless thoughts that eventually come out of their undisciplined mouths.

What are you thinking about? What is your mind-set? How are you developing a mind-set that focuses on the things of the Spirit?

I lived in Berlin, Germany, with my wife for eight months just before the dismantling of the Berlin Wall. Berlin, like many large cities, is a busy and worldly city. We lived in a tiny, run-down, fifth-floor apartment in an impoverished area of the city that still bears the scars of the pounding it received during World War II. Our neighborhood was mostly populated by one Middle Eastern people group. Our plan after we left Berlin was to move to the Middle East, which would soon be our home for the following seven years. So we didn't spend much time studying the German language. Instead, we concentrated on the target language of the country toward which we were heading.

Trudi and I felt about as out-of-place in Berlin as one can feel. We were a couple of lonely young Americans living in Germany, trying to learn a minority language in a host culture that had little sympathy for what we were doing. We weren't yet at ease in the minority culture, and we weren't comfortable in the host culture. There were precious few people nearby with whom we could even talk. Both of us experienced acute loneliness despite the millions of people around us. We missed home, and openly wondered whether our wild-eyed idealism had landed us in a place that would swallow us up.

In the midst of such loneliness, disorientation, and cultural stress I quickly became aware of how important it was to turn my heart toward the things of the Spirit on a moment-by-moment basis. So in addition to daily Bible reading, memorization, and prayer walks, I decided to make composing worship music a part of my regular life. Thus, during a span of only eight months, I wrote some twenty worship songs that I mostly now use just for personal times of worship. Some of those songs ended up being pretty good songs; some of them really aren't all that good. But there would be no way for me to exaggerate how precious those songs are to me today. They are a window into a young soul who kept lifting his eyes up to his loving Lord during a time when it would have been so easy to look down. Whenever I sing them, they remind me of how important it is to keep my mind set on the things of the Spirit, particularly when my circumstances are stressful.

The question, how does one overcome the pull of the flesh? sounds like an old riddle: How can someone extract all of the air out of a drinking glass? A science major at the university where I teach might stay up all night trying to devise an airtight seal for the top of glass that would allow her to pull out all the air from the jar and leave only a vacuum. The same night, an English major who knows nothing about the science major's project could walk into the room, fill the glass with water, and accomplish the same thing. The most direct way to get all the air out of a glass is by filling it with something else.

The way to get rid of "It's a Small World after All" is to replace it with a different song, preferably a spiritual song. You substitute "Amazing Grace" or "Before the Throne of God Above" for "The Song That Doesn't End." And what about that deadliest of all songs, "The Song That Gets on Everybody's Nerves"? You close your ears and turn away your eyes from the things of this world that pull and tug and lure and entice, and instead you:

> Turn your eyes upon Jesus.
> Look full in his wonderful face.
> And the *song that gets on everybody's nerves* will grow
>   strangely dim,
> In the light of his glory and grace.[3]

You cannot simply extract thoughts that displease God from your mind. Like the science major's glass, you need to be filled up with thoughts—indeed with an entire mind-set—that is oriented toward the things of the Spirit. In the last chapter we saw that walking in the Spirit keeps you from carrying out the desires of the flesh (Gal. 5:16). In this chapter, we have seen that thinking about the things of the Spirit will keep you from thinking about the things of the flesh.

In Matthew 16:23, Jesus turns and rebukes Peter using the same verb that Paul employs in Romans 8:5: "Get behind me, Satan! You are a hindrance to me. For you are not *setting your mind* on the things of God, but on the things of man." Are you setting your mind on God's interests? Is your mind set on the things of the Spirit?

So, how do you live life in the Spirit?
1. Walk in the Spirit.
2. Set your mind on the things of the Spirit.

Questions for Review

1. What does the word usually translated as *mind* refer to in Romans 8:5–8?
2. What is the problem with translating the Greek word *sarx* as *flesh*? What is the problem with translating it as *sinful nature*?
3. What is the *flesh* in Romans 8?
4. How do you minimize the pull of the flesh?
5. How does your thought-life relate to overcoming sin?
6. What is the problem with filling your mind with lots of trivial or unspiritual things if you want to live life in the Holy Spirit?

three

PUT TO DEATH THE DEEDS
OF THE BODY BY THE SPIRIT

══

was sitting in my office with one of my students, a soon-to-graduate senior, engaged in a heavy conversation. In a certain sense, this conversation had started for me in the middle of the previous night. I had awakened very suddenly about midnight feeling a deep heaviness and with my mind riveted to the thought that this twenty-two-year-old young man was at that moment doing something that was not pleasing to the Lord. I spent a bit of time praying for him, but ended up going back to sleep with a lasting discomfort about what I had just experienced, especially because I had no idea of what to do with this disturbing thought.

After class the following day—and much to my surprise, because he had never done this before—this young man asked to walk with me back to my office on the other side of campus. He had a theological question, and, although I was trying to responsibly answer his question, I was having trouble staying focused; I was internally deliberating whether God had set up this conversation so I could ask him a pointed question. As the conversation began to wind down, I uttered a short prayer for courage, took the risk, and said: "You know, I woke up suddenly last night around midnight and could not shake the thought you were doing something at that very moment that you should not have been doing. Now I know that I could be really off on this—and *please* forgive me if I am—but at least let me ask you whether there was something going on last night that you should talk to me about."

He looked surprised, but after a momentary pause affirmed that he wanted to talk to me, but alone in my office if at all possible. After sitting down, he took a deep breath and told me that at midnight the previous night he had been alone with a female student, engaged in some kind of sexual behavior. I probed a bit deeper (I have had to learn to probe more in recent years), and asked if this was something he had done before. I was distraught—to say the least—to learn that there had been an ongoing pattern in this young man's life of sweet-talking young women just long enough to get as much from them sexually as they would give before he moved on to someone else.

So here I was in my office listening to a young man admit that he had taken advantage of numerous young women, probably some of whom had been students in my classes. But when I asked him whether he had ever entreated the Holy Spirit to empower him to confess his sin and start living a life of holiness, I was taken aback when he interjected: "Oh, I don't think that's possible." He continued: "So many times in the past I asked the Lord to help me overcome my sinful tendencies, but I was never successful. Eventually, a few years ago I concluded that my expectations for what a Christian life should be were way too high and that I needed to accept myself the way I was and get on with life."

In other words, he was telling me that he was unable to overcome sin—or at least this particular kind of sin—because he had tried so many times in the past to overcome it and had not succeeded. Employing the language of Romans 8, he was essentially telling me that he was *obligated* to the flesh to live according to the flesh. But what if the apostle Paul could talk to this guy? What would he say to him?

> So then, brothers, we are debtors, not to the flesh, to live according to the flesh. For if you live according to the flesh you will die, but if by the Spirit you put to death the deeds of the body, you will live. (Rom. 8:12–13)

The apostle Paul would tell this young man that if he truly was born of the Spirit, he was not obliged to live according to his sinful tendencies. Along with this, he would probably warn him that he was on his way to spiritual disaster if he continued on the path he was walking. But Paul would also challenge him and prod him with the truth that he could truly find life if only he would begin to put to death the deeds of the body by the Holy Spirit.

This issue of *obligation to the flesh to live according to the flesh* (as the NASB translates it) is one of the main differences between a person who has been indwelt by the Holy Spirit and one who has not. The person who has been regenerated (born again) by the Spirit is not *stuck* in sin. By the Spirit, the pull of the flesh can be resisted. On the other hand, the person who does not have the Spirit cannot consistently overcome the sinful pull. Granted, she can break a sinful habit, but it will just show up in another sinful pattern in her life. She stops smoking, but the sin pattern appears somewhere else, in pride, selfishness, or overeating. Not so with the *Spirit*-ual person. The person in whom the Spirit lives can consistently live a life that pleases the Lord when she sets her mind on the things of the Spirit and puts to death the deeds of the body by the Spirit.

I regularly come in contact with people who are sure that they will never be able to overcome the pull of the flesh in some particular area—and I sense that more and more people are arriving at this pessimistic conclusion. Like the student I just mentioned, these individuals tell me that they've tried and tried again to overcome some area of sin in their lives; then, having failed, they conclude that a life of overcoming sin is not what the Bible teaches. To put it bluntly, they have adjusted their theology to fit their experience, rather than holding up the promises and potential laid out in the Bible and adjusting their experience to fit with God's theology!

So before we talk about how to put to death the deeds of the body by the Spirit, let's review what Romans 8 says about the potential in the Christian life—what the person who walks in the Spirit can expect to attain. As one of my teachers used to say, "If you shoot at nothing, you'll hit it every time." What sort of life has God provided for us to live? What is possible in the Christian life according to Romans 8?

- We can live with the knowledge that we are free from condemnation (v. 1).
- We can live as people set free from the "law of sin and death" (probably not a reference to the Old Testament Law, but "from the power of sin that leads to death," NLT) (v. 2).
- We can know that the requirement of the Old Testament Law is fulfilled in us, through what Christ has done (vv. 3–4).
- We can walk according to the Spirit rather than according to the flesh (v. 4).
- We can set our minds on the things of the Spirit rather than on the things of the flesh (vv. 5–7).
- We can live as people who are characterized by peace (v. 7).
- We can live lives that are pleasing to God (v. 8, implied).
- We can live free from the obligation to do the things of the flesh (v. 12).

And these are just a few aspects of the *Spirit*-ual walk that God has prepared for us, the life that Jesus referred to as a life lived "abundantly" (John 10:10). Later in Romans 8, when Paul lists out the tribulations and distresses that might try to separate us from the love of Christ, Paul exclaims: "No, in all these things we are more than conquerors through him who loved us" (v. 37).

Shouldn't we adjust our practice to conform to good theology—what God has revealed about the life he has given to us—rather than adjusting our theology to fit the defeated lives that we stumble through when we fail to walk in the Spirit? Paul wants us to know that it is possible to walk a *Spirit*-ual walk in which we overcome sin. But how is it lived out in normal life?

In the last chapter we focused on one part of the answer to this question: if you want to overcome sin, you must "set your mind on the things of the Spirit." As you redirect your thoughts toward the things of God, you increasingly become a person whose thinking processes are so full of the things of the Spirit that the pull of the flesh lessens. You don't want the ice cream because you have just eaten a perfect meal and you are full!

But having the right mind-set, as important as that is, is not the end of the story. In verse 13 Paul adds these words to the discussion of overcoming sin: "if by the Spirit you put to death the deeds of the body, you will live." If setting your mind on the things of the Spirit is the *pattern* that minimizes the pull of the flesh, putting to death the deeds of the body is the *action* that we do each time a temptation presents itself. Setting your mind on the things of the Spirit focuses more on your *thoughts*; putting to death the deeds of the body focuses more upon your *will*.

"Put to death the deeds of the body" is pretty much the same thing as "say no to sin," but unlike the antidrug campaign among youth many years ago, "Just Say No" by itself will never be successful. *Just* saying no will never allow you to consistently overcome sin. Then what must you do? You must say no *by the Spirit*. Christians have been given the Holy Spirit, who personally empowers them to kill off these "misdeeds of the body," as the expression is sometimes translated. "Just Say No" is like trying to eradicate the termites in your house with a fly swatter; the power of the Holy Spirit is like a superpesticide strong enough to kill the whole colony of critters. "Just Say No" neglects the teaching of these verses that everyone is under obligation to the flesh to live according to the flesh unless they have the Spirit. It is only *by the Spirit* that the action of putting to death the deeds of the body can be consistently achieved.

Mortify the Flesh
In an earlier generation, Christian folk used the term *mortification*. To *mortify* something is an old-fashioned way of saying that you "put it to death." (It has nothing to do with a junior high girl feeling mortified, or ashamed, because her father dresses like a nerd! Nobody is going to die from that type of mortification, but Paul stresses that you will live if, and only if, you mortify the sinful deeds of the body.) I'm aware that English, like every other language, changes over time and that words from earlier generations sometimes simply fall out of use. But I can't help but wonder whether we've stopped using the language of mortification not only because the English language has changed, but also because contemporary English-speaking Christians like life to be easy, and *mortifying* the sinful deeds of the body sounds hard!

The verb tense of "put to death" makes it clear that Paul doesn't have in mind something that you do "once and for all" and then are done. Just as you might have to double-team a big man fifty times in a basketball game, you will be putting to death the deeds of the body time and time again. But why say you're putting it to death if you have to do it again and again?

My high school basketball team had to play against a team that had four tall guys—all between 6 foot 7 inches and 6 foot 9 inches tall! But let's suppose for this analogy that you are playing against a team with only *one* tall guy. What will your much shorter players try to do? They will do all they can to *render ineffective* the big guy. When he posts up, one defender will quickly shift into position just behind him, and another player will front him. When the point guard tries to throw in an entry pass, these two players will sandwich him between their two bodies just long enough for the fronting player to jump up and intercept the entry pass. When they do this correctly, they *shut down* the big man and in effect take him out of the game. He isn't dead, but he might as well be, since in that situation he cannot positively contribute to his team's effort to win the game. So, to "put to death" really means to *render ineffective, something that might need to be done again and again.* Just remember, though, putting to death the deeds of the body is *active*. There is no passivity here.

I grew up in a church setting that was into "higher life" teaching. This teaching goes by many different names, including "victorious Christian living," "the exchanged life," and "the crucified life." A particular stream of higher life teaching that continues to be influential is known as the Keswick Movement (pronounced KES-ik), named after an annual Bible conference that has been taking place in

Keswick, England, each year since the late nineteenth century. One key aspect of higher life teaching is probably traceable even further back to a movement referred to as Quietism, which was popular in Italy, France, and Spain during the seventeenth century. If you aren't familiar with any of these labels, it is still likely that you are familiar with a slogan that gets used in connection with various strands of this teaching: "Let Go and Let God." Said differently, the key to the Christian life is to "let go of reliance on yourself and let God do the work in you."

So much of what is taught in evangelical higher life circles is right and helpful, and I want to affirm much of it. The emphasis on surrendering oneself to Christ, the importance placed upon overcoming sin and living in holiness, and the awareness of the need for empowering by the Holy Spirit to defeat sin, spread the good news, and live a life pleasing to God are all praiseworthy. Higher life emphases have also been affirmed by many who have been catalysts for significant missionary thrusts during the past couple centuries. Actually, the reason it sometimes gets referred to as "higher life" teaching is because these brothers and sisters are unwilling to settle for the mediocrity they see among so many professing Christians. They know that the Scriptures teach something better. On these points, for sure, I could not agree more.

But there exists in the idea of "letting go and letting God do it" an implicit passivity. Surprisingly, many people who strongly emphasize "releasing their wills to God" and "allowing him to do his work in and through them" are not passive at all in their own lives. Nevertheless, a form of passivity is present in their teaching, and the apostle Paul would have nothing to do with it if he were here.

I remember hearing a higher life teacher once use the illustration that you should view yourself like a limp glove into which God puts his hand. The only thing you are to do is surrender yourself to God so that he can do his work through you. But the apostle Paul would disagree. I'll let him speak for himself; then you decide whether he is encouraging passive acquiescence or whether he is active, and encouraging others to be active as well.

> *Do your best* to present yourself to God as one approved, a worker who has no need to be ashamed, rightly handling the word of truth. (2 Tim. 2:15)

> Only let your manner of life be worthy of the gospel of Christ, so that whether I come and see you or am absent, I may hear of you that you are *standing firm* in one spirit, with one mind *striving side by side for the faith of the gospel.* (Phil. 1:27)

> So *flee* youthful passions and *pursue* righteousness, faith, love, and peace, along with those who call on the Lord from a pure heart. (2 Tim. 2:22)

> *Put on* the whole armor of God, that you may be able to *stand* against the schemes of the devil. For *we do not wrestle* against flesh and blood, but against the rulers, against the authorities, against the cosmic powers over this present darkness, against the spiritual forces of evil in the heavenly places. Therefore *take up* the whole armor of God, that you may be able to *withstand* in

the evil day, and having done all, to *stand firm. Stand
therefore.* . . . (Eph. 6:11–14)

Him we proclaim, warning everyone and teaching everyone with all wisdom, that we may present
everyone mature in Christ. For this *I toil, struggling
with all his energy* that he powerfully works within me.
(Col. 1:28–29)

This last verse is especially helpful because it emphasizes both that Christians must toil and struggle, but also
that they must do it with the energy that God works within
us. Similarly, when Paul says in Romans 8:13 that we need
to "put to death the deeds of the body," he emphasizes
that it is to be done "by the Spirit." But remember, such
a statement is not an encouragement to passivity! We
are to actively kill sinful deeds, and that activity is Spirit-
empowered and Spirit-motivated.

Trust and Obey
People from legalistic church backgrounds often find
freedom and learn to deeply trust in the Lord when they
discover the let-go-and-let-God teaching. Learning how to
trust often brings their Christian lives into balance since
they already know well the importance of obedience. But
some then turn around and teach only about trust and
leave out the importance of obedience! Others, like me,
who receive their earliest Christian training in a church
that emphasizes the *trust* aspect of the Christian life, often
come into balance when they learn about radical, obedi-
ent, faithful discipleship. But then they—like I did for so
long—only emphasize forsaking all to follow Jesus in their

teaching, and put little emphasis on the need to surrender to Christ and depend upon the empowerment of the Holy Spirit. I think the hymn writer had the balance right: "Trust and obey, for there's no other way to be happy in Jesus than to trust and obey."[1]

Obedience *and* trust. Action *and* acquiescence. Activity *and* spiritual enabling. Putting to death the deeds of the body *and* being empowered by the Spirit to do it. It is not one or the other. Trust undergirds obedience, and obedience enlivens trust.

It seems that the hang-up for many people is the thought that if they are actively battling sin, then they cannot possibly be trusting in the Spirit. They think that if they are striving hard, then they must be working in their own strength rather than in the strength of the Spirit. I cannot emphasize enough how incorrect such thinking is. Sure, it is possible to do lots of activity—even fighting against sin—in one's own strength and without a dependence upon the Holy Spirit. But this does not mean that we are to be passive. Rather, we are by the Spirit to render the deeds of the body ineffective and not give the devil any sort of foothold in our lives (Eph. 4:27).

So in prayerful trust and continual dependence upon the empowering of the Holy Spirit, we take action so that the sinful deeds of the body aren't given any life. We prepare ahead of time for the day of temptation through prayer, study in the Word of God, and growth in faith (Eph. 6:10–20). We carefully avoid places and situations in which we would be tempted. We call out to the Lord when we are tempted, and stand firm (Eph. 6:13–14) or flee (2 Tim. 2:22), as the situation requires. And if we succumb to a temptation, we do not wallow in our sin, but immediately confess to the Lord that we have sinned, promptly make restitution to any individual that we have wronged, and actively begin to prepare, through the practice of spiritual disciplines, for the next time we are tempted.

In the process, it is important to recognize that certain areas of temptation will require more attentiveness than others. For example, I am not tempted to go out and drown my sorrows in alcohol. But this is no victory for me; I have *never* been tempted in this area, though for you this might be a difficult temptation that will require special attentiveness. I do *occasionally* feel the temptation to use humor to cut down someone else, because in the past I used humor in that way. But I rarely give into it anymore, because it is something that I have surrendered to the Lord repeatedly over the years; I have actively resisted the temptation when I have felt a cut-down about to work its way onto my lips. I still *regularly* am tempted to assert my own selfishness and pride. For example, I could easily find myself tempted to start focusing on how I hope that you like this book (and me as the author), when I really should keep my focus entirely on equipping you to take hold of life in the Holy Spirit so that God will be glorified in you! But I'm aware of those areas of weakness and temptation, and am actively putting them to death by the strength that the Holy Spirit provides.

So the student who sat in my office and told me that he couldn't overcome his sinful passions was wrong. We are called to battle against the sinful desires that wage war with us, in the expectation that we can defeat them by the power of the Spirit. A life lived under the control of the

Spirit is possible, but not if we are passive about it. We must actively put to death the deeds of the body by the Spirit.

So, how do you live life in the Spirit?
1. Walk in the Spirit.
2. Set your mind on the things of the Spirit.
3. Put to death the deeds of the body by the Spirit.

Questions for Review

1. This chapter discusses one significant difference between someone who is indwelt by the Spirit and someone who is not (related to *obligation*). Explain the difference.
2. When people find themselves falling into the same sin over and over again, what sometimes happens to their views and beliefs about victory over sin?
3. Can you "just say no" to sin?
4. What does it mean to *put to death the deeds of the body*? Is this something you do once-and-for-all and then are done with it?
5. What is the problem with the idea of simply *letting go and letting God do it*? What is the relationship between trust and active obedience?
6. Are certain temptations harder for some individuals than for others? How does knowing the answer to this question help you?

four

BE LED BY THE SPIRIT

One day while walking across the campus where I teach, I saw a student from a previous semester standing about fifty feet away from me. His back was turned, and he didn't see me walk by. I offered a short prayer for him as I passed, but after taking a few more steps was unable to shake the thought that I should turn around and go after that young man. I have learned from experience that when I can't let a thought like this go, it is better to do something than nothing, even if I'm not sure what I should do. So I headed back in his direction. When I came up behind him and called his name, he turned around abruptly, and with a startled expression on his face exclaimed, "I was praying this very moment that God would make a way for me to speak with you." We sat down and shared a deeply meaningful hour of counseling and prayer.

Romans 8:14 introduces the next aspect of the *Spirit*ual walk, the leading of the Spirit. Paul writes: "For all who are led by the Spirit of God are sons of God."

Now there is little doubt that the "leading" Paul refers to in this verse means more than what some people mean when they use the expression "the leading of the Spirit." But it certainly doesn't mean less. Paul uses the expression in Galatians 5:18 to describe a generally Spirit-oriented life in contrast to life lived under the Law and the power of the flesh, which is not so different from the general way he uses the metaphor of walking in the Spirit in Romans 8:4 and Galatians 5:16. And the "leading" in Romans 8:14 seems broad enough to include the "putting to death the deeds of the body" we just looked at in chapter 3. But the insistence of a few recent interpreters that Romans 8:14 doesn't include guidance in one's daily experience is unnecessarily restrictive, particularly since such a suggestion doesn't fit the apostle Paul's own experience of sometimes being led more directly, or the example of Jesus in his earthly ministry (see Luke 4:1). Furthermore, early Christians who commented on Romans 8:14 often used it to refer to guidance from the Holy Spirit. And since Romans 8:15–17 (see chap. 5 in this book), 8:26–27 (see chap. 7), and 9:1 all point to other situations in which the Holy Spirit witnesses directly to our spirits, we should not be hesitant to think that more specific guidance by the Spirit is part of what it means to be "led by the Spirit" in Romans 8:14.

What, then, is the Holy Spirit's role in the decisions we face throughout our lives. The short answer for the person walking in the Spirit is that the Holy Spirit *leads* us as we move through the decisions of our lives, whether they are small or major decisions.

This of course begs the question, *how* does he lead us?

How the Holy Spirit Leads

The Holy Spirit leads us broadly (always) and more specifically (sometimes). He always leads us through his written Word, which was revealed to the prophets by the Holy Spirit (2 Pet. 1:20–21). The Bible is the inspired Word of God and is useful in teaching us how to live, correcting and rebuking us when we're wrong, and training us in how to live righteous lives (2 Tim. 3:16–17). We are to prayerfully, carefully, and humbly apply broad biblical wisdom to the situations we face in our lives. This assumes, of course, that we are saturating ourselves in the Word of God—reading it, memorizing it, and meditating on it. Knowing God's Word is foundational to all facets of the Spirit's leading and is the anchor for anything that can be referred to as *leading*. (This cannot be too strongly stressed!) Furthermore, when we face a situation in which we still do not know what to do, we can ask for an *increase* of wisdom, which God has promised to give us when we ask in faith (James 1:5–6).

But the leading of the Holy Spirit doesn't always stop there. The Holy Spirit *sometimes* puts forward more direct communication in various ways, as the Bible records again and again. Now I am aware that there is a significant group of biblical interpreters who think that this more direct aspect of the Spirit's leading is not available to us today. Some of my past teachers and present colleagues believe this. But a person who takes this position must also assume that the many dozens of times in the Bible where God instructs someone to leave and go somewhere else (for example, Abraham in Gen. 12:1; Elijah in 1 Kings 18:1; Cornelius in Acts 10:5; and Paul in Gal. 2:2), or when he puts something into their hearts or minds to do something (as with Nehemiah in Neh. 2:12 and 7:5 or Paul in Acts 20:22), *must all be special cases, limited to a different time/era/age and situation* rather than experiences that constitute some sort of pattern. In contrast, I believe that God can and still does lead in these ways today, though I don't know of anywhere in the Bible where the claim is made that God will *always* do so for every decision we make. But that doesn't mean we shouldn't stay open to him *sometimes* leading in these ways—all the while being ready to move forward using biblically-rooted wisdom when God chooses not to guide in a more direct manner.

Even though I am happy to attest to many instances when I have received more direct guidance from the Holy Spirit—and will give you a few examples of these on the pages ahead—there have also been many decisions that my wife and I have taken based solely upon biblically-rooted wisdom in conjunction with the mission and ministry we have received from the Lord. These have included both smaller decisions about how and where to invest time in ministry as well as larger decisions such as whether to pursue graduate studies or to move to a different city. But even wisdom-based decision making should be considered part of the Holy Spirit's leading for the one who lives life in the Spirit.

But since God does sometimes guide more directly, and since direct guidance is a little more difficult to grasp (no less to explain!), let me spend a bit more time discussing and illustrating this more direct aspect of the Spirit's leading. My hope is to encourage you to be sensitive to his leading when he does choose to move in this way.

I was walking from my home toward campus (my fifteen-minute "commute") and praying about the day ahead when I remembered a comment that I had made to a female student a few days before that could easily have been taken as hurtful. When I had first uttered the comment, it hadn't even crossed my mind that it could have been hurtful, but as I prayed about it during my walk to school I became increasingly convinced that I needed to do something about my error. That very day I located the student and confessed my unkind word to her. She was gracious in her response, but also appreciative that I had said something about it. I believe that this was an example of a more direct leading of the Holy Spirit, beyond a simple application of biblical wisdom. I believe that it was the Holy Spirit who brought that comment to mind as I was praying that morning.

Though we need to be ready to make decisions based solely upon biblically-grounded missional wisdom, we also need to intentionally develop a sensitivity to a more direct leading of the Spirit. Then when he brings to mind a wrongdoing of which we were not aware (compare Ps. 139:23–24 and Phil. 3:15) or prompts us to speak to someone in need (like the student I mentioned at the beginning of this chapter), we will be ready and available.

Let me assure you, though, that you will not wake up some morning and suddenly be sensitive to this aspect of the leading of the Holy Spirit. You can't take a pill that will make you responsive to his guidance, and although many people wish otherwise, you can't simply have people lay their hands upon you so that you instantaneously become Spirit-sensitive. The process takes time and practice.

I once watched a television documentary about hearing aids and a therapy developed for those who use them. People who experience hearing loss appreciate the help they get from a hearing aid's amplification. But in a crowded room, say at a party, hearing aids apparently are often quite frustrating for their users because *all* the noise in the room is amplified, not just the voice the listener wants to hear. The diversity of sounds makes it difficult to pick out the particular voice that needs to be heard.

But according to the documentary, there is a therapy for this problem. A patient listens to and views a crowded, noisy virtual room on a computer. He must pick out one particular voice from across the virtual room. The only difference from real life is that whatever is spoken by the person across the room is also written in words on the computer screen. Apparently, if someone uses this therapy regularly, he or she can learn to pick out what someone is saying even when other conversations are taking place at the same time.

What a wonderful analogy for learning to pay attention to the Spirit! Attentiveness to the written Word sensitizes us to the ways the Spirit works, to his priorities, and to his patterns. Then, with time and experience, despite all the noise of life (that is, everything that is trying to lead our minds away from a sincere and pure devotion to Christ, 2 Cor. 11:3), we become accustomed to distinguishing the Spirit from other thoughts whenever the Spirit chooses to lead in this manner.

Sheep Know the Shepherd's Voice

But someone might ask: "What does it *feel* like to be led by the Spirit in this way?" I'm afraid that I cannot easily answer that question. Some spiritual things that are *real* are not easily communicated through concrete language. How does one describe the taste of a clementine to someone who has never tasted one? (Clementines are my favorite fruit; it looks a bit like a tangerine but is seedless and much sweeter.) How does one "taste and see that the LORD is good" (Ps. 34:8)? Perhaps the best that can be done is to compare it to something familiar. That's actually what Paul may be doing in Romans 8:14. Many commentators suggest that the best analogy for the "leading" in this verse is that of a shepherd and his sheep. In other words, observe how sheep relate to their shepherd and you can understand to some extent what it means to follow the Spirit's lead. In the Bible, God is regularly compared to a shepherd who leads his sheep. Here are three examples. (At some point you should read the entire chapters where these verses are found, since each has a lot more about the Lord as Shepherd.)

> The LORD is my shepherd; I shall not want.
>   He makes me lie down in green pastures.
> He leads me beside still waters.
>   He restores my soul.
> He leads me in paths of righteousness
>   for his name's sake. (Ps. 23:1–3)

For thus says the Lord GOD: Behold, I, I myself will search for my sheep and will seek them out. As a shepherd seeks out his flock when he is among his sheep that have been scattered, so will I seek out my sheep, and I will rescue them from all places where they have been scattered on a day of clouds and thick darkness. (Ezek. 34:11–12)

But you do not believe because you are not part of my flock. My sheep hear my voice, and I know them, and they follow me. I give them eternal life, and they will never perish, and no one will snatch them out of my hand. (John 10:26–28)

By analogy, just as sheep learn to listen to the voice of their shepherd and follow, we also need to learn to be led by the Holy Spirit in our lives. Perhaps the most important thing we can do to develop sensitivity to the Holy Spirit's guidance in addition to saturating ourselves in the Word of God is to spend blocks of time in prayer before the Lord. Talk to him conversationally. Ask him questions; expect answers. Take your time; don't rush. Learn to pray "in the Spirit" (see chap. 7), and let the Holy Spirit guide you into the types of things you should pray about. As you pray, if you think that the Holy Spirit is impressing upon you that you need to be doing something in particular, or need to be praying about something in particular, spend more time on that point. Talk to your friends and spiritual counselors about it. Then step out and begin to act, staying sensitive to the Spirit's redirection. You certainly can't expect more guidance from the Holy Spirit if you are unwilling to act on what you think he is impressing upon you, even if what you are being called to do isn't easy.

I wrote early notes for this chapter from a retreat center in the mountains. I went there for an extended period of prayer before starting this book. As I prayed, I had a distinct sense that I needed to talk to my family about joining me in a dedicated time of fasting and prayer about an upcoming event that would affect us all. Since fasting before important decisions is modeled in the Bible (see Acts 13:1–4; 14:23), my sense that we as a family should do this was nothing out of the ordinary (at least as far as the Bible is concerned). But I do believe it was *by the Spirit* that I realized this would be a good thing to do in that particular instance.

The Holy Spirit leads us broadly (always) and more specifically (sometimes). The Bible teaches us the ways of God and how to apply those ways to our lives. Sometimes the Holy Spirit leads us more directly. This doesn't mean that he always leads this way. The Holy Spirit can choose to act in any way and according to any timetable that he wishes; we do not dictate to him how or when he will move. But since the Bible gives many examples of him acting more specifically, we should anticipate that he will sometimes choose to lead us more directly if we are open and available to his guidance.

A few years ago, one of my university colleagues and I were invited to a "young scholars" breakfast hosted by a large Christian publishing house. During the previous year or so, my colleague and I—without telling anyone else—had begun discussing the possibility of writing or editing a book together about the way the New Testament authors quote from and allude to Old Testament passages. But we hadn't yet done anything about it, and we were certainly not ready to talk to anyone about it.

But it just so happened (better put: the Holy Spirit so arranged it) that my colleague and I were across from each other at the same round table where the editor-in-chief of the publishing house was commenting on a type of book that he wanted to publish, which was the same type of book we were interested in writing. My colleague made quick eye contact with me, but there was nothing to say or do, since he was just about to launch into an important conversation with a different editor. As formal and informal conversations broke out at all the tables, I looked up at a young woman standing alone across the room who had been introduced a few minutes before as a new editor at this publishing house. (I don't think any of us knew her before that day.) At that moment, I felt very strongly in my spirit that I should talk to her about our book idea. But I couldn't do it without the permission of my colleague who was at that moment in the middle of "pitching" his other book. But the sense that I should speak with her was so strong that I got up out of my chair, interrupted my colleague, and whispered in his ear, "Do you mind if I share our idea about the book on the Old Testament in the New Testament with this woman over here?" And surprisingly, he agreed. I promptly introduced myself and shared our idea with her. She enthusiastically affirmed the idea, and proceeded to invite me and my colleague to join her for lunch to talk about it. Before the lunch was over, we had an informal agreement that we would do this book!

The following day my colleague ran into this same editor at a book exhibition. She pulled him aside and said, "You won't believe it! Only an hour ago, another New Testament scholar approached me and presented me with the same idea you proposed yesterday. I told him that it was a great idea, but that we couldn't do it since that project was already underway." And would you believe it, a few weeks later, an entirely different person sent a formal proposal to the same publishing house on a similar idea? If my colleague and I had not acted in that moment, we might never have had the opportunity to produce that book. In retrospect, the two of us look back and see the leading of the Holy Spirit written all over that situation!

Of course, it is sometimes clearer *after the fact* that the Holy Spirit was moving in a particular instance! But each time we respond to the Spirit's promptings and receive confirmation that it was in fact the Spirit, we become increasingly able to discern what the Spirit is doing and more confident to ask for his guidance.

Soon after my wife and I arrived in the first of two cities in which we lived in the Middle East, we began to realize that what we had been told about reaching Muslims with the gospel might not be such good advice. The conventional wisdom at that time (and in many circles today) was that the way to introduce people to Jesus in the Middle East was the same as what you would do in your neighborhood back home: befriend them, live a life of integrity before them, and invite them into your home. Eventually—so went the conventional wisdom—they might open up to you and to your Lord like people sometimes do back home.

The problem was that in the Middle East our neighbors and friends were friendlier than we were, and my wife and I are pretty friendly people! They were—at least outwardly—quite moral people, and because of their long history of Middle Eastern hospitality, almost all of them were more hospitable than any American Christian we'd ever met. On these standards, there was nothing unusual about our lives, so it was rather unlikely that we'd reach people that way. We continued to show love and hospitality to our Muslim friends and neighbors throughout our years overseas, but we soon came to realize that this was not how they would be primarily reached.

But one day as I walked through this largely unreached city of two million people, I thought about all the people who were praying for us—hundreds of pray-ers daily lifting their voices up to God on behalf of those we were coming in contact with. Even with the tiniest bit of faith, I could believe that one person in a thousand in this city was open to the good news in answer to their prayers! Do the math. In a city of two million, that meant that there would be two thousand people open to the gospel in that city. Our ministry strategy from that day forward was simple: find them!

Without going into the rest of the story, life from that day onward became a running prayer that God would lead my wife and me to people whose hearts he had already been opening to himself. Each day I would pray: "Lord, guide me to the people you have prepared. I will speak up when you bring me in contact with them. And show me what else I need to do to find other precious souls within whom you have already begun a work by your Holy Spirit." My journals are filled with stories of how he did this.

Child of God, may you be led by the Holy Spirit! May he lead you to people with whom you need to speak and convict you of areas that aren't pleasing to the Lord. May he draw you to places of ministry that he has prepared for you and guide you in the decisions of life. And may the active presence of the Spirit in your life be one of the ways that you know that you are a child of God, as our verse says: "For all who are being led by the Spirit of God are sons of God" (Rom. 8:14).

So, how do you live life in the Spirit?
1. Walk in the Spirit.
2. Set your mind on the things of the Spirit.
3. Put to death the deeds of the body by the Spirit.
4. Be led by the Spirit.

Questions for Review
1. How does the Holy Spirit lead us as we move through life? What does the leading of the Spirit include?
2. How important is knowing the Word of God in the discussion of the leading of the Spirit?
3. Some Christians believe that direct guidance from the Holy Spirit doesn't ever occur in this age. This chapter contends that it sometimes does. What do you believe about this, and why?
4. Why is it difficult to describe to others how the Holy Spirit leads?
5. Do you agree that it is sometimes easier to see the guidance of the Holy Spirit after the fact than before? Can you think of any examples from your own experience?

KNOW THE FATHERHOOD
OF GOD BY THE SPIRIT

═══

Recently a loving family in our church finally adopted a little boy. I say "finally" because it took three years for this adoption to finalize! The county department of child and family services had him removed from a home that was characterized by fear and neglect, and placed him with a family that dearly wanted to adopt him. But a process that normally takes twelve to eighteen months stretched into more than thirty-six months. But finally that little boy stood before a judge with his new mommy and daddy and was officially and finally adopted by a family that loved him. I wasn't there, but I can imagine the scene:

The adoption lawyer walks over to the boy and asks, "Are you ready?" The boy nods. The lawyer and the boy approach the judge together and immediately are joined by the eager parents who take a seat next to the boy in the front row. The judge looks at the boy and asks: "Do you want this man and this woman to be your forever mommy and daddy?" The boy looks up at the judge with hopeful eyes and exclaims: "Yes. Forever and forever." Then, as the judge declares the adoption final using a lot of big words, the boy glances at the face of the adoption lawyer to be sure that it is all for real, then jumps into the arms of his forever daddy, reaching over at the same time to grab his forever mommy so he can hug them together as hard as he can. He cries out: "I love you, Mommy! I love you, Daddy!" His parents, with tears filling their eyes, engulf him in hugs and kisses and tell him once again how much they love him, and that he will forever be their child, and that nothing is going to change that now.

God the Father adopts us as his children—how amazing is that? And the Holy Spirit is the agent by which we receive that adoption, through whom we cry out in love to the Father, and by whom we know for certain that we are children of God:

> For you did not receive the spirit of slavery to fall back into fear, but you have received the Spirit of adoption as sons, by whom we cry, "Abba! Father!" The Spirit himself bears witness with our spirit that we are children of God, and if children, then heirs—heirs of God and fellow heirs with Christ, provided we suffer with him in order that we may also be glorified with him. (Rom. 8:15–17)

Without the Holy Spirit, we would never know what it is to find freedom and identity as God's adoptive children.

But thankfully, God has freely given us his Holy Spirit, and these verses from Romans 8 display three amazing things that the Spirit does. First, he acts as the go-between who takes us out of a place of slavery and fear and brings us into a place of adoption and acceptance. Second, he helps us to cry out to God as Father. And third, he testifies with our spirit that we are children of God. Let's spend some time on each of these ideas.

The Holy Spirit Takes Us from a Place of Slavery and Fear to a Place of Adoption and Acceptance

Scripture portrays us as formerly living as slaves who cringed in fear of intimidating masters. As we saw in chapter 3, we were at that time under obligation to the flesh (Rom. 8:12). That obligation is described here in Romans 8:15 as nothing short of slavery! We were completely in bondage and unable to get ourselves out of the situation. Only someone else could release us from such a place of fear.

And that's what the Holy Spirit has done. His indwelling in our lives means that he is the agent through whom the very Lord and Creator of the universe has adopted us out of slavery into his family! "You did not receive the spirit of slavery to fall back into fear, but you have received the Spirit of adoption." When Paul uses the expression "you have not received a spirit of slavery," it is unclear whether he means that we have not received the kind of *attitude* a slave would have, that is, cringing in fear at his master, or whether he means that we have not received an evil spirit who enslaves us and causes us to be afraid. But in either case, Paul's emphasis is not on that expression at all; his emphasis is on the Holy Spirit of adoption whom we *have in fact received*. And the *Holy Spirit* isn't an *attitude*, since the very next line says that he is the agent by whom we cry out in love to our adoptive father, and an attitude isn't an agent of anything.

So we are no longer in slavery, and we no longer have to live with the fear that goes along with being slaves. We are in an adoptive relationship with God the Father, and this has been accomplished through the Spirit. We do not have to live in fear anymore! We have been officially transferred out of a place in which fear reigns and put into a secure and loving family with a Father who is strong enough to protect us from all that would seek to harm us, and wise enough to know the best way to do it!

The Holy Spirit Helps Us Address God as "Father"

Since we have received our adoption, the Holy Spirit helps us, motivates us, and empowers us to cry out in thankfulness and love toward God with the expression "Abba, Father!" Perhaps when Paul wrote this, he was thinking about the hesitancy that someone who came out of the bondage and fear of slavery might have in fully accepting his adoption. By the help of the Holy Spirit, we learn to cry out in trusting thankfulness to God for adopting us and making us part of his family.

People often say that the Aramaic word that Paul uses here, "abba," simply means "daddy," something that a little child would call out. This misunderstanding was popularized by German scholar Joachim Jeremias who wrote, "Abba was an everyday word, a homely family-word. No Jew would have dared to address God in this manner."[1] But this is not entirely accurate. "Abba" really isn't a straight equivalent to "daddy"; probably a better translation is "father."[2] (And there is literature before the time of Jesus where God is addressed by Jewish people as father.[3]) The reason that "father" is probably the better translation is because it carries both an *element of intimacy* and an *element of respect* at the same time.

We find Jesus crying out to God as Abba in the heart-wrenching but extremely submissive words in Mark 14:36: "Abba, Father, all things are possible for you. Remove this cup from me. Yet not what I will, but what you will." You can detect both the intimacy and the submission in his words. And if we were to back-translate the "our Father" at the beginning of the Lord's Prayer (Matt. 6:9) from Greek into Aramaic—the language Jesus used for teaching—it probably would come out as "Abba." But the next words in the prayer, "in heaven" and "holy is your name," show both intimacy and reverence.

Is it really possible for *intimacy* and *respect* to exist at the same time? Absolutely yes! I remember talking one evening with my daughter, Grace, on her bed when she was around ten years old. She had just become aware of the very distressing truth that some children are afraid of their fathers—and for good reason—and she wanted to talk about it. Part way through the conversation, and knowing full well how she would respond, I asked her, "Grace, are you afraid of me?" Without hesitation, she gushed, "Oh, no, Daddy! I'm not afraid of. . . ." She stopped midsentence and proceeded much more seriously, "But when I do something wrong, I'm afraid." Here was my daughter, who would jump into my arms whenever I came in the door or lovingly snuggle with me while I read a book to her, also relating to me as the father who disciplined her—albeit in love—when she did something wrong. She knew how to relate to me both with intimacy and respect. If such a combination is possible in a relationship between a fallible earthly father and his daughter, surely it is possible between a perfect heavenly Father and his adopted children.

But what does the Holy Spirit have to do with this? How does he have anything to do with our addressing God as Father? Romans 8:15 says, "But you have received the Spirit of adoption as sons, by whom we cry, 'Abba! Father!'" How does the Holy Spirit do that?

Fortunately, Galatians 4:1–7 is so similar that we can get some insight from there about what Paul probably intends in Romans 8:15. In Galatians 4:1–7 Paul discusses our release from slavery and our adoption as God's children. But verse 6 reads: "And because you are sons, God has sent the Spirit of his Son into our hearts, crying, 'Abba! Father!'" In Galatians, the Holy Spirit has been sent into our hearts and *he* is the one who cries "Abba! Father!" whereas in Romans *we* do it *by* the Spirit. Because of the close similarities between the two passages, I think it is likely that they are looking at the same activity of the Spirit from two different perspectives—one from the perspective of what *we* are doing by the Spirit (Rom. 8:15) and one from the perspective of what the *Spirit* is doing in us (Gal. 4:6). That is, *we* cry out in acknowledgment of our adoption *along with* the Holy Spirit who is crying out with us. We cry out at the same time as he is crying out! But more than that, he is doing this in order to encourage us and strengthen us to receive and fully accept that God is our Father. He is interceding *with* us and *for* us at the same time, just as we will see him doing in prayer when we get to Romans 8:26–27. This is also somewhat similar to Romans 5:5: "And hope does not put us to shame, because God's love has been poured into our hearts through the Holy Spirit who has been given to us." The Spirit's own action and encouragement help us—we who cower in fear because of our past enslavement—to know the love of the Father and to relate to God as Father. The Holy Spirit pours out his love toward us and toward the Father so that we might also pour out our love to the Father. We join in overflowing thankfulness with the Holy Spirit that God has adopted us as his child!

The Holy Spirit Testifies with Our Spirit That We Are Children of God

How can we know we are children of God? Part of the answer to this question is that the Holy Spirit does a direct work upon our human spirit by which he communicates to us and through us that we are children of God. Other places in Scripture probe whether we are in fact continuing in faith and whether there is fruit in our daily lives that points toward genuine faith (Matt. 7:15–20; John 15:1–16; 2 Cor. 13:5; Col. 1:21–23). But Romans 8:16 is concerned with a direct work of the Holy Spirit upon our human spirit by which we can know that we are part of God's family.

There is some discussion among biblical scholars about whether Romans 8:16 should be understood as the Holy Spirit communicating *to* our spirit the truth that we are children of God, or whether it should be understood as the Holy Spirit testifying *with* our spirit to God that we are children of God. But in light of what we have already seen regarding the Holy Spirit crying out "Abba, Father" to God along *with* us, our thinking is probably too much either/or when we ask this question. Since we have just seen in the previous verse that the Holy Spirit is probably crying out alongside of us, and at the same time encouraging us in our crying out to acknowledge that God is our Father, it seems likely that Romans 8:16 is continuing the same thought.

Here it would be the Holy Spirit testifying alongside of us—and in this way testifying to us—that we are children of God. For if the Holy Spirit is acknowledging to the Father that we are his children, and we are doing it *with* him, then we are also receiving in our spirit confirmation that we belong to him. Thus, the Holy Spirit is testifying *to* our spirit even as he testifies *with* our spirit to God. This *testifying* (or *bearing witness*) is simply a declaration and acknowledgment of the truth that we are children of God, just as we saw in verse 15.

Romans 8:16 has become so very precious to me during the past few years! My mother, whom I love dearly and who has had a significant impact on my spiritual life, has been afflicted for many years now with Alzheimer's disease. She has what is known as early-onset Alzheimer's, a disease that began showing signs when she was in her midforties. It has been a long and difficult road for her and for my dad who has lovingly cared for her for many years. I have often experienced a sense of helplessness in regard to my mom, since I live so far away from her (almost one thousand miles) and since there is little I could do to improve her situation even if I were closer. Do you know how I have been praying for my precious mom since I came to realize the significance of this verse for her? I ask the Holy Spirit to "bear witness with her spirit that she is a child of God." My mom may not have a mind that functions very well, but I believe that the Holy Spirit can do a direct work on my mother's spirit and confirm to her—in spite of her confused mind—that she is a child of God. I sincerely believe that the Lord has heard me and answered this prayer over and over again. And I look forward to asking my mom how he did it when I get to talk to her once again after she has received a resurrection body and a renewed mind.

What a remarkable thought this is! Each of us who truly knows Christ is reminded by the Holy Spirit over and over that we are adopted members of his family! What freedom could come to each of us if only we internalized this truth!

I grew up with both a father and a mother who genuinely loved me, prayed for me, and wished the best for me. It is natural for me to relate to God as my Father, since I know what it is to share both intimacy and respect for my earthly father. But I know many people who have great difficulty relating to God as their Father. When I taught at a Christian college in New York, I knew a young man who had a great struggle with accepting the love of his heavenly Father and relating to him as his Father because his earthly father was alcoholic and abusive. It was only as this young man began to learn to relate to God as Father through the Holy Spirit that he was able to break through into a consistent life of holiness. As the Holy Spirit kept working on his spirit, he grew more and more to understand this crucial and freeing truth. As a result, he is no longer bound to the slavery and fear that he carried from his childhood into his young adulthood, for he knows in truth that God is his loving father and he openly receives and acknowledges that truth. And when he finds himself discouraged or doubting God's care and providence in his life, he reminds himself of this life-changing thought—that the God who spun the universe into existence has lovingly adopted him into his family as his forever child and, as Romans 8:17 says, has given him an inheritance alongside of Jesus Christ!

But many of us spend our days "listening" to criticisms that bounce around inside of our heads and allow them, rather than God's Word, to form the way we view ourselves. Throughout the day, we might "listen" to hundreds of such criticisms and reinforce them because we repeat them to ourselves over and over again. We tell ourselves the things we have heard in the past, such as:

"You never get anything right. You're always making mistakes."

"Nobody wants to be your friend. Why would anyone want to be a friend with *you*?"

"You're the reason your family is so messed up. They would have been better off without you."

"You're stupid, and everybody knows it."

"You're never going to amount to anything. Your life is a waste."

"What's the matter with you?"

Christian man or woman, stop listening to these words! Our identity is formed by what *God* thinks of us, what *God* has done for us, and what *God* intends to do with us, not by anything else. You and I need to turn off these destructive messages and start listening to what God says about us.

So what has God said about us in Romans 8 up to this point? Every line I list here is taken directly out of Romans 8:1–17:

> We are not under condemnation.
> We are not debtors to the flesh.
> We have been indwelt by the Holy Spirit.
> We belong to Christ.
> Our spirits are alive.
> We are children of God.
> We are adopted into his family.
> We are coheirs with Jesus Christ.
> We will be glorified together with him.

Why don't you go back over this list and speak these truths out loud to yourself, asking the Holy Spirit to solidify them in your own spirit? And if you need to, why don't you do this every day, or even multiple times throughout the day? If you're really serious about changing the messages you're listening to, you could begin adding to this list truths you find from other places in the Bible that describe what God has done for you and how he sees you. Meditate often on these truths so that you begin believing them. Can you see how freeing this might be?

I know that many of you have trouble getting rid of the criticisms of your past. But you are a child of God! This is simply something you need to receive, because it is true. It is truer than anything you have ever been told in your life. I tell it to you on the authority of the Word of God.

You are a child of God and will receive an inheritance with Jesus Christ. Believe it!

Can you imagine how different your life would look if your actions were not driven by the negative thoughts that constantly barrage your mind? Can you imagine how different life would be if your life were characterized by a heart full of thankfulness to God that you are his child, an attitude of prayerfulness that the Holy Spirit would keep confirming this to you, and a boldness in the authority you have as his child to attempt great things in his name? What an astonishing thing it is that God has chosen you to be his child!

As I began putting together thoughts for this book, God was quietly doing a work in the hearts of my wife and me. Three times previously we had prayed about adopting more children (we have two biological daughters, Lydia and Grace), but had decided against it because of the ministries we were already involved in and because of future hopes for ministry. But during the time I began working on this book—the fourth time my wife and I seriously prayed about this issue—God was peeling open our hearts so that we would begin pursuing adopting children out of the Los Angeles foster care system. The children in that system have often been abandoned by or taken away from their biological parents and are in desperate need of a loving family. Little did we realize how we would come to know the fatherhood of God toward us as his adopted children during this period! Actually, one of our stated reasons for adopting children was because of the dual themes of God's care for orphans in the Old Testament and of our adoption as God's children in the New Testament. But no passage has impacted me more personally on this topic than Romans 8:15–17.

My heart has expanded as I've grown to understand the astounding love of God toward me. I have thought long and hard about God's sacrifice of his own Son to make a way for me to share in his eternal inheritance. I have thanked God more than at any other time in my life that he chose to adopt me, not because of anything I have done, but because of his incredible mercy. I have become aware of how God placed his love upon me even before I knew he existed. I have been awakened to my desperate plight had God not shown me his grace. And sometimes, I find myself crying out to God, "Abba! Father! What an amazing thing you have done!"

Just as I was finishing work on this chapter, we received a call from a social worker telling us they had found two girls (two lovely and precious girls—ages eight and ten), who really needed a home and family. After bathing it in prayer, we agreed to bring them into our home and to adopt them as soon as the county cleared us to do so. And this all happened before they even knew we existed! Imagine how much my wife and I have been impacted in thinking about God's choice to set his love upon us, not on the basis of anything that we have done, but simply because he chose to make us his children. Immediately upon entering our home, my heart was about to burst with love for Graciela and Ana and for my heavenly father who has given them to us. Oh, how much my thankfulness toward God has grown, and my confidence in addressing him as Abba Father, and my knowledge that I truly am his child. The presence of these girls reminds us every day that God has made us his own children through adoption. My prayer is that *you* may come to know this incredible gift of adoption that you have received from your loving heavenly Father and that has been imparted to you by his Spirit. May you deeply come to know that God is truly your Father! May you learn to *walk* in light of that reality.

So, how do you live life in the Spirit?
1. Walk in the Spirit.
2. Set your mind on the things of the Spirit.
3. Put to death the deeds of the body by the Spirit.
4. Be led by the Spirit.
5. Know the fatherhood of God by the Spirit.

Questions for Discussion
1. How does understanding your spiritual adoption work against fear?
2. What is the role of the Holy Spirit in helping us to address God as "Father"?
3. Does "Abba" simply mean "Daddy"?
4. How can we know we are children of God, and what does the Holy Spirit have to do with it?
5. What changes can take place in a Christian's life when he or she learns how to relate to God as Father?
6. How is a Christian's sense of identity formed? How does knowing the answer to this question help you deal with past criticisms that you still "listen" to?

six

HOPE IN THE SPIRIT

—

In chapter 2 I described the radical life reorientation I experienced at age fourteen when I started thinking about eternity. Let me tell you a little more about that. From age five onward, my father, who came to the Lord when I was five, and my mother, who reaffirmed her faith at the same time, taught me about Jesus. I soon embraced their faith as my own. With the exception of a short period during junior high school, Jesus was a regular part of my life. Even during junior high school, I read my Bible regularly, though some of my reasons for doing so were not the best. But it was during the first year of high school when God really grabbed my heart.

On a few sporadic nights over the course of about two months, I read my Bible before going to bed, turned out the light, and tried to fall asleep. But on each of these nights

I couldn't sleep. I began thinking about eternity, and my thoughts wouldn't let go of me. In a spirit of prayer—hour after hour—the eyes of my heart turned upward and I truly began to believe that eternity was real and that life on earth was short in comparison. As I look back over those precious nights, I believe that the Holy Spirit was riveting my attention to thoughts of eternity, putting the hope of heaven deep in my heart, and impressing upon me the futility of life lived without eternal purpose.

I never got over it. Thoughts of the brevity of life and one day being with the Lord continue to grip me. I deeply long to be with Jesus in a resurrected body and free of this fallen and twisted world. Things that appear important to other people often strike me as trifling and inconsequential, because I can't stop thinking about eternity with my Lord Jesus and how short the present life is.

I also experience *longings* that I haven't always known what to do about. Sometimes these longings are strong enough that I experience them as *groanings*. I feel them most keenly during periods of suffering. Though they are somewhat difficult to describe in words, I think they arise out of the stark contrast between what I *hope for* and the reality of life in a deeply fallen world.

Longing for Something More

Do you ever feel like you don't quite *belong* in this world—that you don't exactly fit? Ever since I began to think about eternity, I have felt this way over and over again—probably hundreds of times now. I can't tell you how much this discomfort with the present world used to bother me. I guess I assumed that if God put me here, then I shouldn't always be thinking about the future. I was much like a child who has been taken for a special day to the seashore to play on the beach but who spends his day wishing he were at an amusement park. I now know that there is nothing wrong with these pangs of longing, and that, in fact, these are important in the Christian life, as C. S. Lewis commented: "A continual looking forward to the eternal world is not (as some modern people think) a form of escapism or wishful thinking, but one of the things a Christian is meant to do."[1]

Early in Romans 8 Paul pointed his readers toward the future, and in particular, toward what we will experience in the resurrection of our bodies. I skipped these verses earlier because this book focuses on walking in the Spirit. But these verses belong here in our discussion of future hope. Paul writes:

> You, however, are not in the flesh but in the Spirit, if in fact the Spirit of God dwells in you. Anyone who does not have the Spirit of Christ does not belong to him. But if Christ is in you, although the body is dead because of sin, the Spirit is life because of righteousness. If the Spirit of him who raised Jesus from the dead dwells in you, he who raised Christ Jesus from the dead will also give life to your mortal bodies through his Spirit who dwells in you. (Rom. 8:9–11)

Paul is emphatic that if we are indwelt by the Holy Spirit, we can know that we belong to Christ and that one day God will raise us from the dead and give us resurrection bodies through his Holy Spirit.

After verses 9–11, Paul lays out three things we need to do in our lives in the Spirit: (1) put to death the deeds of the body by the Spirit (Rom. 8:12–13, see chap. 3 in this book); (2) be led by the Spirit (Rom. 8:14, see chap. 4); and (3) know the fatherhood of God by the Spirit (Rom. 8:15–17, see chap. 5). At the very end of the section about knowing God as Father, Paul introduces the contrasting themes of present suffering and future glory:

> And if children, then heirs—heirs of God and fellow heirs with Christ, provided we suffer with him in order that we may also be glorified with him. (Rom. 8:17)

Then Paul breaks wide open the theme of suffering in the midst of a fallen world and couples it with the longing of creation:

> For I consider that the sufferings of this present time are not worth comparing with the glory that is to be revealed to us. For the creation waits with eager longing for the revealing of the sons of God. For the creation was subjected to futility, not willingly, but because of him who subjected it, in hope that the creation itself will be set free from its bondage to corruption and obtain the freedom of the glory of the children of God. For we know that the whole creation has been groaning together in the pains of childbirth until now. (Rom. 8:18–22)

When Adam and Eve ate the clementine (who says it was an apple?), it was not only their human descendants who were affected; God also subjected the *creation*—that is, all the lower things God created besides human beings— to *futility* or *frustration*. Remember that the judgment God pronounced in the garden of Eden included a curse against the "ground" (see Gen. 3:17–19). In Romans 8:18–22 Paul personifies inanimate creation and describes it as waiting in anticipation—even groaning—until the day the children of God are glorified and the rest of the world can be set free from its bondage. Every time I read this passage, I think of the Disney version of the fairy tale *Beauty and the Beast* where the candlesticks, clocks, teapots, and even the wardrobe longingly wait and suffer, groaning and hoping, until the beast is loved by the beautiful maiden and the beast's curse is removed along with theirs. Imagine that! Like the inanimate objects in *Beauty and the Beast*, all of creation is pictured as groaning with longing! Why should I be surprised that I don't fit perfectly in this world and that I find myself yearning for a place that is better by far?

Our Longings and the Holy Spirit

Now we come to the section where the Holy Spirit and our longings are brought into the picture:

> And not only the creation, but we ourselves, who have the firstfruits of the Spirit, groan inwardly as we wait eagerly for adoption as sons, the redemption of our bodies. For in this hope we were saved. Now hope that is seen is not hope. For who hopes for what he sees? But if we hope for what we do not see, we wait for it with patience. (Rom. 8:23–25)

Hope. What an amazing word! Unfortunately it has lost much of its *oomph* in the way we use it in daily life. Look at three examples:

"I hope life will improve after I move to a different city."

"She is hoping against hope for a change in her exam grade."

"We hope to join you tonight, but we think there is too much to get done at home."

In each of these statements, hope is not so different from the word "wish." It is desire for something to happen even though there really isn't much expectation that what is hoped for will actually occur.

Biblical hope is nothing at all like that! The biblical concept represented by the English word "hope" is so strong that it is almost a synonym for "eager expectation." And the focus of the expectation isn't that life will get better here; it is absorbed with the glorious life to come. For this reason, I sometimes wonder whether we ought to start using the word "expectation" or "anticipation" in place of "hope" in order to get back the *oomph* that is usually lost when we talk about hope. Such expectation shows up three times in this section of Romans 8:

The creation waits with eager longing. (v. 19)

As we wait eagerly for our adoption as sons. (v. 23)

We wait for it with patience. (v. 25)

Are we waiting eagerly—not passively, but with eager longing—the glorious future that God has prepared for us? Why is it that we talk so little about this today in our churches? Have we lost the longing for the future? Have we mislaid the urgency that comes from acknowledging how short our lives are in comparison to an eternity yet to be revealed?

Three aspects of this glorious future show up in verse 23:

- *We will share in a full harvest of glory*, even though we only know it partially now through the presence of the Holy Spirit. That is what the expression "the firstfruits of the Spirit" indicates. Just as the Israelites were commanded to bring the first part of the harvest to a celebration in anticipation of the coming harvest (Lev. 23:9–14), so we have received the first installment of our glorious future in the indwelling presence and power of the Holy Spirit.
- *We will receive our final adoption.* This doesn't mean that we aren't already adopted as his children. We are, and Paul told us so a few verses earlier (Rom. 8:15–17). But just as some of the glory of the future gets pulled into our present lives through the Holy Spirit's indwelling presence, so we who have been adopted into God's family are still awaiting the final adoption celebration.
- *Our bodies will be redeemed.* Just as we have been redeemed already, there is a final resurrected body that will be given to us that is glorious (Phil. 3:20–21).

But what is the role of the Holy Spirit in all this? Romans 8:23 says: "We ourselves, who have the firstfruits of the Spirit, groan inwardly as we wait eagerly for adoption as sons, the redemption of our body." This verse says something astounding, even surprising. Paul claims that it is *because* we have the Spirit, not *despite* it that we groan. Paul doesn't say: "Oh, you're suffering, but the Holy Spirit will alleviate your sufferings." No, in this passage, it is precisely the presence of the Spirit within you that causes you to feel this particular kind of suffering—the longing for final redemption in the midst of a fallen world—so acutely! Let me offer a couple analogies for how something so good (here, the presence of the Holy Spirit) can sometimes be the catalyst for painful longing (here, for our future redemption).

My second year out of high school, I attended college seven hundred miles away from my home town. As with many young college students, I experienced significant homesickness. I shed more than one tear when I thought about my family. Actually, it was *because* I loved my family so much that I grieved the distance between us.

In early November, my parents surprised me by sending me an airplane ticket so I could come home for Thanksgiving break. I kept those tickets on my desk in my dorm room, looking over at them regularly, because they represented reunification with my family. Those tickets produced in me eager expectation of what was coming while at the same time they brought painful longings to the surface. They represented both hope and groaning at the same time. Similarly, we groan and we hope because the presence of the Holy Spirit in us causes us to long for a wonderful future that is coming soon.

Toward the end of my third year of college, I sang a song in which I proposed to my sweetheart Trudi on a little beach beside the Sandy River in Oregon. I pulled an engagement ring out of my guitar case and put it on her finger. And best of all, she said yes!

Unfortunately, just over a month later we had to begin a long summer apart from each other. Both our parents wanted us home for the last summer before marrying and leaving for who knows where! So I spent the summer in the Bay Area in California while Trudi passed her summer in Southern California, four hundred miles away. And although Trudi's parents and sister lived in Southern California, they had only recently moved there, so the "home" she stayed in was a place she had never lived. She didn't have any friends in the area, didn't know the people in the church she attended, and spent the summer taking care of other people's children. Her situation was like Romans 8:23–25 in a number of ways. She was engaged—with a ring to prove it—but not yet married, and was living at a distance from her loved one (me!). The ring represented incredible joy at what had already occurred as well as hope at what was to come—just as the presence of the Holy Spirit does in our lives—but it was also the very thing that caused her to "groan" because every time she looked down at her finger the ring reminded her that her surroundings were not what she wanted them to be and that she would rather be with me!

Romans 8 uses yet a different illustration for the groanings, that of childbirth (v. 22). The very contractions that communicate hope to a mother that she will soon bring a child into the world are also what bring her the most immediate pain.

The presence of the Holy Spirit in our lives reminds us of the stark contrast between the wonderful things God has prepared for us who believe and this fallen world that is so full of sin, suffering, and futility. As a result, we sometimes "groan"—and rightly so—with longing for a better day in the future.

Now where does hope—or *eager expectation*—come from? Should we just try really hard to get it? No, like all the other Christian virtues (or "fruit," see Gal. 5:22–23) like love (Rom. 5:5) and faith (Rom. 12:3), hope is something that the Holy Spirit is actively seeking to fill us with. Romans 15:13 makes this clear: "May the God of hope fill you with all joy and peace in believing, so that by the power of the Holy Spirit you may abound in hope." But we can cooperate with the Holy Spirit's desire to increase hope in our lives by thinking a lot about heaven and regularly contrasting life here with life then. Paul does this *all the time* in his letters (see, for example, 2 Cor. 4:16–5:10; Phil. 1:19–26; and Col. 3:1–4). And he does it here in Romans 8:18 as well: "For I consider that the sufferings of this present time are not worth comparing with the glory that is to be revealed to us."

How often do you think about the glories that are yet to come? Do you habitually ponder the relationship of future glory to present suffering? Are you cooperating with the Holy Spirit who is seeking to produce in you yearnings for the future, or are you suppressing those longings? Or even worse, are you drowning them out because of an entertainment addiction or the pursuit of happiness in a fleeting and transitory world?

Edward Burman was my dorm roommate during one of my years at college in Portland, Oregon. Edward had grown up in Laramie, Wyoming (his favorite word was "mosey"). Edward had two passions. He loved to ride his bike. He had taken bike treks across the United States and Europe. In fact, he used to ride his bike everywhere, even to class when it was just across the campus. His other passion was for Jesus. Edward loved the Lord, spending large amounts of time in prayer and memorization of Scripture, and he was hoping to become an overseas missionary.

But Edward had a rare degenerative disease called olivopontocerebellar degeneration, including optic atrophy, a disease that people can easily confuse with Lou Gehrig's Disease (ALS). Areas deep within his brain just above his spinal cord were shrinking. When I first met Edward, I couldn't tell that anything was wrong with him except that his eyesight was bad. But by the second year of college, when he was my roommate, Edward began to have trouble with his balance and motor skills. He started to experience small mishaps on his bicycle. As time progressed his speech slurred, his handwriting got worse, and he often had to hold onto something when he walked—like a doorframe or a wall. It was not unusual to see Edward, all 6 feet 5 inches of him, trip on something and end up sprawled in a heap on the ground.

I remember how excruciating our discussion was the night I talked him into putting away his bicycle for good. He openly wept about that loss many times.

But Edward was studying the Word of God and hoping that God would open a way for him to go into overseas ministry. But no mission would take him. By now he was too sick. So he changed the focus of his ministry and became a prayer warrior and supporter of all of his friends who did have the privilege of serving overseas.

He moved back to Wyoming and received monthly government assistance for a place to live, for a special computer, and for a walker and a wheelchair. During all seven years that my wife and I lived in the Middle East, he supported us for $50 a month out of his tiny government stipend. I think he sent us more than $8,000 all together during those years. And it was only later that I learned that we weren't the only ones he was supporting. I think Edward was my most faithful supporter and prayer partner during my years overseas.

A few years ago, Edward choked to death because his swallowing skill had been compromised by his disease. He is now with the Lord.

Don't get me wrong; it wasn't easy for Edward. I remember the desperation that he sometimes expressed at his loss of control and independence. And I have read excerpts from his journal that show how deep a valley he sometimes walked through. But Edward kept looking up out of the shadow of death into the light of the glory yet to come. Whatever else may be said about my roommate and friend, I am confident that Edward lived each day in light of eternity. He knew where his destiny lay and ordered his life in such a way that his values reflected his beliefs about the future. He groaned in his body—as all of us should— while he awaited the glory that would someday be his. He groaned because the presence of the Spirit reminded him of the disparity between his transient existence and the glories yet to come. He knew his life was short and kept reminding those around him that their lives were short, too! By the power of the Holy Spirit he lived in hope of eternal glorification, final redemption, and forever being with the Lord. And now, Edward knows the glory that he hoped one day would be his in the presence of his Lord.

So, how do you live life in the Spirit?
1. Walk in the Spirit.
2. Set your mind on the things of the Spirit.
3. Put to death the deeds of the body by the Spirit.
4. Be led by the Spirit.
5. Know the fatherhood of God by the Spirit.
6. Hope in the Spirit.

Questions for Discussion

1. How can thinking about eternity impact the way you live your life?
2. Should a Christian feel completely at home in the world? Are longings for the world-to-come good or not?
3. What is the difference between the way many people use the word *hope* and biblical *hope*?
4. What is the Holy Spirit's role in the longings we feel for the future?
5. Where does hope come from? Do you simply *try hard* to have hope?
6. What difference does hope make in a fallen world that includes a lot of suffering?

PRAY IN THE SPIRIT

During my first year of marriage, my new bride and I financially lived on a shoestring. She was finishing up her last year of college and I was working two jobs to pay the bills. We were actively ministering in a Southeast Asian refugee community in Portland, Oregon, into which we had moved for that very purpose. We cared far more about ministry and getting ready for future church planting than we did about living a comfortable lifestyle. But that didn't mean we never had any financial concerns.

One of my jobs was working on the "box line" at United Parcel Service. I would wake up at around 3:00 a.m. every morning, drive fifteen miles in our little Toyota Tercel, load boxes into trucks for five hours, and then drive home. If you don't know what a Toyota Tercel is, just think of the smallest car on the road and imagine that its frame is made out of tinfoil. But we were quite at peace with our one little car, until the day the heater lever stopped working. The problem wasn't with the heater; it was with the control lever on the heater. I could push the lever to the left (cold), but when I pushed it toward the right (hot), I couldn't get it past the middle point. As a result, there was no heat in the car. It was November, and I began to imagine a long winter driving on moist and frigid winter mornings in an unheated car to an unheated warehouse and back to our apartment again in an unheated car.

I took the car to a local auto shop, and got a quote for $170 to fix the lever. The amount might as well have been $2,000; coming up with $170 at that time in our lives was not an option. So Trudi and I took our need to the Lord in prayer. We didn't really know how to pray specifically; we just laid out the concern to a God we knew was our loving heavenly Father.

We then experienced one of the most loving examples of God's persistent grace we have ever experienced. I went down to my car the next morning, turned the ignition key, and then reached over to push the heating lever to the right. It moved into place and I was able to heat the car all the way to work. This happened, despite the fact that I had not been able to move the lever for the previous three weeks! When I came out of work five hours later, the sun had come up and the day was warming considerably, so I moved the lever to the left again. But no sooner had I done so than I realized that it was stuck again and would not go back into the heating position. We again brought the need to the Lord in prayer, and when I started the car at 3:00 a.m. the next morning, I once again got heat.

For the rest of the time we owned that car, about another year (including the entire Portland winter), God graced me with heat by allowing the lever to move to the right every morning I got into the car. But whenever I moved the lever to the left during the warmer parts of the days, the lever would get stuck!

Trudi and I remember this series of events—in our minds an ongoing miracle—as a pile of gracious acts of a loving God who heard the prayer of a young couple who needed him to intervene. We didn't really know how to pray, but we knew that the Holy Spirit was moving us to pray and helping us as we prayed.

Pray with Sensitivity to the Spirit

Only a couple years before these events, when I was a college student, I went through a period in which I struggled a lot with the promises in Scripture about God answering prayer. My biggest problem was with Scripture passages in which Jesus or one of the apostles offered wide-open promises, such as:

> Whatever you ask in my name, this I will do, that the Father may be glorified in the Son. If you ask me anything in my name, I will do it. (John 14:13–14)

> If you abide in me, and my words abide in you, ask whatever you wish, and it will be done for you. . . .You did not choose me, but I chose you and appointed you that you should go and bear fruit and that your fruit should abide, so that whatever you ask the Father in my name, he may give it to you. (John 15:7, 16)

And this is the confidence that we have toward him,
that if we ask anything according to his will he hears
us. And if we know that he hears us in whatever we ask,
we know that we have the requests that we have asked
of him. (1 John 5:14–15)

As I struggled to understand these verses, I also longed
to know the reality of these promises in my own prayer
life. But because I had grown up in a church that was
somewhat allergic to the Holy Spirit, it took me quite a
few years to begin to appreciate the central role the Spirit
plays in our prayers. Simply put, the person who experiences the blessing of answered prayer is the person who
is sensitive to the guidance of the Spirit as he or she prays.
As children of God, our responsibility is to learn to pray
"in the Spirit" (Eph. 6:18; Jude 20) so that what we pray
for is in accordance with the will of God.

Frequently the Bible, and especially Paul's letters, use
the expression "in the Spirit"—or expressions that are quite
similar. This kind of expression is used in various con-
texts and situations, but the one we're most interested in
here is when people are described as *doing things* "in the
Spirit." What kinds of activities are people doing *in the
Spirit* according to the Bible? People are:

- proclaiming the gospel in the Spirit (Mark 13:11;
  Acts 1:8; Rom. 15:19; 1 Cor. 2:4, 13; 1 Thess. 1:5);
- growing in love and unity toward each other in the
  Spirit (Acts 9:31; Eph. 4:3; 2:22; Phil. 2:1–2; Col. 1:8);
- seeing visions or being "carried" somewhere in
  the Spirit (Ezek. 11:24; 37:1; Rev. 1:10; 4:2; 17:3;
  21:10);

- living in righteousness, peace, and joy in the Spirit (Rom. 14:17; 15:13; 1 Thess. 1:6);
- being led or hindered from going somewhere by the Spirit (Luke 2:27; 4:1; Acts 16:6–7; 19:21);
- prophesying in the Spirit (Matt. 22:43; Mark 12:36; Luke 2:27–35; Acts 11:28; Eph. 3:5; see Joel 2:28–29; Acts 2:17–18; 21:4; 20:23; 21:11; 1 Tim. 4:1).

But equally or perhaps more pronounced than any of these is some form of *praying* in the Spirit. Here are some examples.

Blessing God in the Spirit

Otherwise, if you bless *in the Spirit*, how can anyone in the place of an outsider say "Amen" to your thanksgiving when he does not know what you are saying? (1 Cor. 14:16, AT)

And he came *in the Spirit* into the temple, and when the parents brought in the child Jesus, to do for him according to the custom of the Law, he took him up in his arms and blessed God. . . ." (Luke 2:27–28)

Rejoicing in the Spirit

In that same hour he rejoiced *in the Holy Spirit* and said, "I thank You, Father. . . ." (Luke 10:21)

Worshiping by the Spirit

For we are the real circumcision, who *worship by the Spirit of God* and glory in Christ Jesus and put no confidence in the flesh. (Phil. 3:3; see also John 4:23)

Praying to God in the Spirit

But you, beloved, build yourselves up in your most holy faith; pray in the Holy Spirit. (Jude 20)

> Praying at all times in the Spirit, with all prayer and supplication. To that end keep alert with all perseverance, making supplication for all the saints. (Eph. 6:18)

This last one is especially important because many New Testament scholars suggest that prayer "in the Spirit" in Ephesians 6:18 is shorthand for what Paul describes in Romans 8:26–27:

> In the same way the Spirit also joins to help our weakness; for we do not know what we should pray for, but the Spirit Himself intercedes with wordless groanings. And the Spirit who searches hearts knows the mind set on the Spirit, because he intercedes for the saints according to the will of God. (AT)

What the Spirit Does When We Pray

These two verses are so rich and helpful in our lives in the Spirit! I have probably spent more time on these two verses than any other verses in the Bible during the past two years. Because of how significant this passage is for understanding a life of prayer, let me draw out a few of the more important ideas.

First, we learn that we are weak when we come to prayer ("in our weakness"). Moreover, we learn that we often don't know specifically what to pray for in any given situation (something we already know from experience!). The Greek expression is literally: "for the *what* we should pray just as it is necessary we do not know." The concern is not about the *manner* of prayer (the "how"), but rather the *content* of our prayers—what do we actually pray about? These verses do not teach that we are always completely in the dark when we pray, as some of our English translations suggest, but rather that we often do not know the specifics of how to pray in any given situation. For example, when we pray for a brother who has cancer, should we pray for healing, or for wisdom for the doctors, or for grace to endure to the end?

Second, and gloriously, we learn that the Spirit joins to help us when we are weak and when we are struggling to know how to pray by interceding for us with wordless groanings. It is not, as some propose, that we should just pray whatever we want since we don't have any idea how to pray, and that the Spirit—in some way disconnected from us—takes our prayers-in-the-dark, fixes them up, and prays on our behalf to the Father. Rather, the verb often translated as "helps" has a preposition attached to the front of it, which suggests that it really means "joins to help," as some translations render it. And in light of the idea Paul already introduced a few verses earlier—that the Spirit *comes alongside of us* to cry out in thankfulness to the Father for adopting us and *testifies alongside of us* that we are children of God (see my comments in chap. 5 of this book on Rom. 8:15–17 and Gal. 4:1–7)—we should understand this verse to mean that the Spirit comes alongside to help us to pray and then presents our requests to the Father. The early church theologian Augustine put it this way: "The Holy Spirit, who intercedes with God on behalf of the saints . . . moves us to pray when we groan, and thus he is said to do what we do when he moves us."[1]

Third, the Holy Spirit does this with "wordless groanings." Once again, this shows that the Holy Spirit is joining us in our prayers since our groanings (see Rom. 8:23) have been taken over by the Spirit (v. 26). The Holy Spirit joins our groanings, making them his own, and intercedes with these wordless groanings to the Father. Despite the popularity in some circles of the idea that this is a reference to speaking in tongues, there is no indication in the passage of this, particularly since these groanings are described literally (in the Greek) as "wordless," and tongues are spoken.

Fourth, in the midst of this, the Spirit is searching our hearts ("he who searches hearts") and knows that we have a mind-set that is focused on him ("knows the mind of the Spirit"), even if we do not know exactly what we are supposed to pray.[2] As a result, when he intercedes before the Father on our behalf, he knows both parties in the intercession: he knows what is in our heart, and he knows the will of the Father.

Fifth, the result is that our prayers are prayed "according to the will of God" because the Holy Spirit is moving us thus to pray and is presenting the prayers that he is guiding us to pray (in accordance with the Father's will) to the Father. This is what it is to "pray in the Spirit" (Eph. 6:18). One who prays according to the way the Spirit is guiding will be praying in accordance with the will of God, and so can expect his prayers to be answered.

One of the most dramatic examples I ever witnessed of this process at work occurred during the first year I lived in the Middle East. At the time we were living in a large city that had only one congregation made up of perhaps fifteen Muslim-background believers in Jesus. During the time we lived in this particular city, we would gather with a few ministry coworkers for about four hours of prayer each week. These times of prayer were often visited by the power and presence of the Lord and are precious in my memory. But I'll never forget the time that a single woman—I'll call her Rose—who had lived in this country for about ten years and who was very sensitive to the things of the Spirit, told us that she sensed that we ought to be praying that some people would be baptized that coming summer. "I'm not sure exactly how to pray yet," she said, "but I am moved to pray. Would you pray along with me about this?"

We agreed. But we were really taken aback when the following week she said, "I cannot get out of my mind that we ought to be praying that *ten* people will be baptized this coming summer. Will you pray with me for ten people?"

"Ten people?" I thought, "Doesn't she know where we're living? Doesn't she know that no more than two or three people at a time have *ever* been baptized in this country? Doesn't she know that there are only a total of fifteen Muslim-background believers in the entire city of two million and that this church has existed for more than ten years? It's like a church of 150 people in the United States leading 100 people to Christ and baptizing them all in five months! No, it's much harder than that! This isn't exactly America's Bible Belt!"

These are the thoughts that initially ran through my mind. The thoughts that followed were more sober. I pondered, "Rose is a spiritual woman who doesn't throw ideas against the wall just to see if they'll stick. She obviously has been praying a lot about this and thinks that the Spirit is guiding her to pray for ten people to be baptized in the name of Jesus this next summer. I may not yet have faith to pray for this, but I'm willing on the basis of her faith to begin praying alongside of her." Others must have come to the same conclusion—despite the seeming audacity of the prayer—and agreed to start praying with her about this.

Now, for the sake of full disclosure, you should know that we were aware of two believers in the fellowship who were considering being baptized. So, assuming that they followed through (not a given!), we needed to pray for eight more.

So week after week we brought this request to the Lord, and week after week, those of us who were praying began to increase in faith. A few weeks later, I had the opportunity to be one link in a chain of relationships that culminated in a man coming to faith in Christ, my first such experience in the Middle East. And then a second man I was spending time with believed, and then a third. Each of them wanted to be baptized as a sign of their faith in Christ. Along the way someone else led a woman to Christ, and then someone else; and then a woman came to faith in a nearby village; and then a woman who had just come to Christ moved into our city wanting to be baptized. When the day came, there were *nine* people from Muslim backgrounds who came to the beach ready to be baptized. But, there was also one long-time believer who had been holding out on baptism who decided right then and there in conversation with the local pastor to get baptized.

I was there. I witnessed *ten* people follow the Lord in baptism in answer to Rose's prayer—and in answer to ours as well, since we had joined her week after week to pray as the Lord increased our faith. This was a phenomenally encouraging day for the local church and for the work of

Christ in that city. Not all of them have stayed faithful to Christ—such is the case with work in that part of the world—but I witnessed a dramatic example of the Spirit guiding a humble and sensitive woman to pray that God would do what nobody at that time imagined could happen.

Charles Spurgeon, the powerful English preacher, described this process as well as anyone I've heard:

> Should we not wait upon God in prayer; asking Him to reveal to us what those matters are concerning which we should plead with Him? Beware of hit-and-miss prayers. Never make haphazard work of intercession. Come to the throne of grace intelligently, understanding what it is that you require.
>
> We feel secure when the Holy Spirit guides our minds. But many spiritual people consciously feel themselves boxed in regarding certain matters, and are free to pray in only one direction. Let them obey the Holy Spirit and pray as He directs, for He knows what our petitions should be. Pray for what the Holy Spirit moves you to pray, and be very sensitive to His influence.[3]

Yes, let us become increasingly sensitive to the influence of the Holy Spirit and receptive to the way that he is guiding us to pray so that our prayers become increasingly aligned with the will of God.

But this is not the way most people pray. Sure, we sometimes don't know what to pray for—Romans 8:26 makes this clear—but this doesn't mean that we shouldn't be attentive to whatever guidance the Spirit may want to give (in his own timing and way) in how we should pray.

How Should We Pray?

Most people I know simply pray for whatever they want to have happen. This issue of praying in the Spirit according to the will of God isn't even on their radar. I just received an e-mail requesting prayer from a secretary at our university about one of our adjunct professors (whose name I've changed). It reads: "Joe fell this weekend while hiking and broke his right arm. Please pray for him as he sees the orthopedic doctor . . . pray for a quick and complete healing."

Now, how do we know that we should pray for a quick and complete healing? Despite how much we want to be able to dictate the nature and content of our prayers, doesn't that prerogative belong only to God?

The pressure to just pray for what we want to have happen intensifies when someone close to us asks us to pray for a precious loved one to be healed from some difficult illness or injury. Of course we should agree to pray for them, but *what* should we pray? Should we pray for healing? How do we know that God wants to heal a person? For reasons only he knows, God does not always choose to heal in this world.

Instead, we need to become sensitive to pray in the way the Spirit is guiding, waiting on his timing and praying in a way that we believe would bring greatest glory to him. Since this is difficult to see how it works out in practice, I've laid out a chart to try to make clear what might occur when a person prays in dependence upon the Spirit.

Of course, those are some of the paths you could go down if you are praying "in the Spirit." Negatively, you could pray with wrong motives, including offering prayers that are driven by selfishness or pride. In such cases, you probably will not receive any guidance from the Spirit (and even if he did guide you, you wouldn't know it!), and you very likely will not see an answer to your prayers. Having said that, God can do *anything* he wants to do, and he may choose to positively answer your prayer in order to humble you by his grace and draw you by his love, or discipline you as his child by giving you what you asked for and letting you feel the weight of receiving something for which you should not have asked. But I made the chart to show you the ways your prayers might proceed as you pray "in the Spirit" and seek to pray according to God's will.

Child of God, may you pray in the Spirit according to the will of God, and depend upon him to lead you as he sovereignly deems best! May you know the power of prayer and the joy it is to cooperate with the Spirit's guidance as you pray. And may God shake the world through the prayers you pray in dependence upon him! Almost every spiritual writer I have ever read on the topic of prayer has emphasized the importance of seeking to pray according to God's will and has focused upon the central role that the Holy Spirit plays in the process. Let me be honest, I am surprised and even amazed at how few people in our generation even realize that praying in sensitivity to the Spirit is even an issue.

In chapter 4 I mentioned a time I spent away in a cabin, during which I mostly prayed, but also during which I wrote down a few notes to incorporate into this book. I also wrote a song from Romans 8:26–27 to use during my own times of worship and in my family worship. This is

Possible Scenarios When You Seek to Pray "in the Spirit" according to the Will of God

What the Holy Spirit Does	What You Do	What Happens	Timing
The Spirit guides you in how you should pray about a given situation.	You are receptive to the Spirit's guidance and faithfully pray in accordance with the guidance he is giving you at the time.	You witness the thing for which you prayed take place.	The process is quick (sometimes even immediate).
The Spirit gradually increases your wisdom about how to pray in a particular situation.	You are receptive to what he is doing, and over a longer period of time become increasingly convinced that you should pray in one particular direction. You pray in that direction.	You see the thing for which you pray *eventually* take place.	The process is gradual (sometimes over a very long time).

my own prayer for the work of the Spirit in prayer. (The two parts can be sung as a round.)

> Spirit I come, not knowing what to say
> Spirit I come, and needing help to pray
> Spirit I come, but my weaknesses are getting in the way
> Spirit I come
> Help me as I pray.
> Search my heart, Lord, know my mind
> In my weakness join to help me
> Wordless groanings,
> Spirit intercede for me
> Help me as I pray.

What the Holy Spirit Does	What You Do	What Happens	Timing
The Holy Spirit sees that the request you are bringing is not in accordance with God's will and begins redirecting you to pray in a different direction.	As you wait in prayer, you come to believe that you are praying in the wrong direction about the issue and you change the way you direct your prayers.	The thing you initially prayed about does not occur, but you are at peace about it since God has redirected you to pray about this situation in a different way.	The process is sometimes quick and sometimes gradual.
For reasons known only to him, the Spirit chooses not to guide you in how to pray in a particular situation. (He is not obligated to give you such guidance, and will sometimes choose not to.)	You continue to wait upon the Lord in prayer, expressing what it is you desire, but also asking him to guide you—if that is his will—so that you can pray in faith.	The thing for which you prayed does *not* take place. You never learn why (at least in this life), but trust that the Spirit knows that your heart is directed toward him and knows best how to intercede for you.	The process remains open-ended.

So, how do you live life in the Spirit?

1. Walk in the Spirit.
2. Set your mind on the things of the Spirit.
3. Put to death the deeds of the body by the Spirit.
4. Be led by the Spirit.
5. Know the fatherhood of God by the Spirit.
6. Hope in the Spirit.
7. Pray in the Spirit.

Questions for Review

1. Have you ever struggled with Jesus's bold promises to answer prayer? Explain.

111

2. When you don't know what to pray for, what does the Holy Spirit do?
3. How does the Holy Spirit help you pray according to the will of God?
4. How should you pray when there is something specific you wish the Lord would do?
5. Why does God sometimes choose not to answer prayers the way you want them to be answered?

THREE UNDERCURRENTS
IN ROMANS 8

═══

his book is about how to live life in the Holy Spirit. It follows the order and topics found in Romans 8, an incredibly rich passage that is arguably the most important chapter on the Holy Spirit in the entire Bible. Since this is a book about how to walk the "*Spirit*-ual walk," it skips a lot of wonderful things found in Romans 8 in order to focus on the Holy Spirit's ministry in the lives of believers. But there are three undercurrents running beneath the surface of Romans 8 that are good to know even though I don't really discuss them in this book. Knowing about these three streams will help you understand Romans 8 better.

*Undercurrent 1: Romans 8 is not just about you and me;
it is also about the change from the old age to the new age.*
Have you ever read a verse out of one of Paul's letters and wondered whether he was writing about your old life

before you were converted, or whether he was writing about the period in which the Old Testament was written? Or say in a different verse, have you ever wondered whether Paul was discussing your new life now that you have been converted to Christ, or whether he was discussing the period of the New Covenant now that Christ has come? The answer to this difficulty is that throughout Romans 8—and in lots of places in his letters—Paul has in mind *both* the change from the old age to the new age *and* the change from a person's old life before coming to know Christ to his new life in Christ. The two ideas are closely related for the apostle; he seamlessly moves back and forth between the two ideas, and even when he is emphasizing one, the other is often implied even when it is not stated directly.

In other words, Romans 8 does focus upon the work of the Holy Spirit in the individual believer, but it also addresses the change from the old age to the new age. It won't do to emphasize only the personal change from one's old life to one's new life. Nor will it do to minimize the application to the individual—as has been in vogue among some recent New Testament scholars—and try to make Romans 8 only about the change from the old age under the Law to the new age under the Spirit. (In other words, some claim that this passage doesn't have much to do with you personally; they say it is *only* about the change between ages.) But such a suggestion fails to appreciate a *fundamental analogy* that permeates Paul's letters—and Romans in particular. Paul is working on two levels and sometimes clearly connects the two. A foundational change has taken place because of the coming of Christ between the old age of the Law and the new age of the Spirit. In direct analogy, a fundamental change has taken place as a result of you leaving your old life and receiving a new life through faith in Jesus Christ and the indwelling of his Spirit. Your old life corresponds to the old age of the Law; your new life corresponds to the new age of the Spirit. Remembering this will help you understand Romans 8 so much better!

Undercurrent 2: Romans 8 starts with an emphasis on the Holy Spirit, but eventually moves toward an affirmation of the security of the believer.

Even though a majority of Romans 8 focuses upon the work of the Holy Spirit in the believer, by the end of the chapter the movement is toward the glorious affirmation that nothing can separate us from the love of God which is in Christ Jesus our Lord. In other words, precious brothers and sisters, we have been chosen from ages past to be conformed to Jesus Christ; there is not a thing in the world that can stand against us when God is for us; no one can bring a successful charge against us; no one has any right to condemn us; and nothing can separate us from the love of Christ (Rom. 8:28–39). The theme of the security of the believer glimmers in some earlier verses, but is blazing in intensity and dazzling in brilliance by the end of the chapter. This book focuses on verses 1–27 of Romans 8, since those are the verses where Paul concentrates on the ministry of the Holy Spirit. But remembering where Paul is ultimately heading in the chapter will help you to more fully understand Romans 8.

Undercurrent 3: Romans 8 is closely connected to what Paul has already written in the book of Romans up to this point.

Paul is making conscious connections with what he has already written in Romans up to this point. In fact, you can almost summarize what has already been taught in Romans from statements sprinkled throughout Romans 8. We are reminded that:

- God sent his own Son in the likeness of sinful flesh (v. 3).
- He allowed his Son to die on the cross as an offering for sin (v. 3).
- He raised Christ from the dead (v. 11).
- He broke the power of sin so that we are no longer under condemnation (vv. 1–3, 12).
- He took care of the Law's requirement (v. 4).
- He regenerated us, making our dead spirits alive (v. 10).
- He broke our obligation to live according to the flesh (v. 12).
- He secured for us a future resurrection with Christ and glorification with him (vv. 11, 17).
- He gave us his Spirit!

Everett Harrison comments on how Romans 8 ties in with the previous three chapters:

> Actually, the chapter gathers up various strands of thought from the entire discussion of both justification and sanctification and ties them together with the crowning knot of glorification. Like ch. 5, it presents the blessings of the justified life, grounded in the removal of condemnation. Like ch. 6, it stresses freedom from the bondage of sin and ultimately from the bondage of death. Like ch. 7, it deals with the problem of the flesh . . . , finding the solution in the liberating and productive ministry of the Spirit. . . .

> This is high and holy ground indeed for the Christian pilgrim to tread.[1]

High and holy ground indeed! If you keep in mind that Romans 8 doesn't stand alone—that it is running in currents that have already been introduced in the earlier chapters of Romans—you will read Romans 8 much more richly. This will also keep you from viewing life in the Spirit as something that is simply mystical or ethereal. The *Spirit*-ual walk is rooted and grounded in the theological truths of what Christ has done, and if Paul could talk to you he would make sure you understood that.

So keep in mind the connections in Romans 8 to what Paul has already written in Romans to this point. But also keep in mind that when Paul gets to the topic of the Holy Spirit in Romans 8, although he has already mentioned the Spirit in passing a few times to this point (Rom. 1:4; 2:29; 5:5; 7:6), he steps it up not just one notch but about *one hundred notches* in Romans 8! Can you imagine what Paul's letter to the Romans would be like if Paul had passed directly from Romans 7 to Romans 9? What an incredible loss this would be to our understanding of the ministry of the Holy Spirit in the lives of those who believe! Yet many Christians live without any sort of clarity about how to live life in the power of the Holy Spirit. Since Romans 8 is the gravitational center of Paul's teaching on the Holy Spirit—and perhaps the gravitational center of the entire Bible's teaching on the Holy Spirit—much of our understanding of how to walk in the Spirit necessarily comes from Romans 8. But don't forget to read it in light of everything else he has already written about in Romans 1–7!

If you will keep these three "undercurrents" in mind as you study Romans 8 on your own, you will find your study of that chapter to be much richer!

Questions for Review
1. Is Romans 8 about the change from the Old Covenant age to the New Covenant age, or is it about the change from our personal lives apart from Christ to new life in Christ? (Or is there another alternative?)
2. What is the main topic Paul discusses in the first twenty-seven verses of Romans 8? What topic does Romans 8 increasingly move toward by the end of the chapter?
3. Is Romans 8 connected with the chapters that come before it, or is it pretty much separate from what comes before?

Appendix 2

HOW TO REMEMBER
WHAT YOU'VE LEARNED

══

One helpful thing you can do to grow in your life in the Spirit is to memorize the seven aspects of life in the Spirit discussed in this book. If you do this, you will possess a handy summary that you can use to remind yourself of central aspects of living life in the Holy Spirit. Here's an easy way to remember these seven points using hand motions. This is also a fun way to teach these points if you ever have the opportunity to teach others about life in the Holy Spirit!

1. *Walk in the Spirit:* Pump your arms at your side and move your feet in a walking motion.
2. *Set your mind on the things of the Spirit:* Point with your index finger to the side of your head three times, indicating your mind-set.

3. *Put to death the deeds of the body by the Spirit:* Make a fist with one hand and hold your other hand below it with the palm open and facing upward. Bring down your fist upon the upward facing palm three times.

4. *Be led by the Spirit:* "Grab" onto a rope with both hands and move both hands out in front of you as though you are holding on and being pulled by that rope.

5. *Know the fatherhood of God by the Spirit:* Bring your hands together in front of you like you are hugging someone. It will be easiest to move to the next motion if you have one open hand covering one hand that has a fist in it for your "hug."

6. *Hope in the Spirit:* Move both hands at the same time toward your chest, one hand covering the other hand which is in a fist. Bring it against your chest three times. (Indicating longing and hope in the midst of suffering.)

7. *Pray in the Spirit:* Place the palms of both hands together with fingers pointing upward in the traditional prayer hand position.

If you can memorize this list—and it will be easy to memorize if you use the hand motions—you will be reminded of each of the main points regarding your relationship to the Holy Spirit in Romans 8, and you will have it as a reminder to live it out. If you decide to teach using this method, introduce each new hand motion as you bring in each new point. Then, just before you transition to the next point, review the points you have already covered using the hand signal—and encourage everyone to do it with you! At the end of point seven you will review all seven. Everyone will enjoy the mnemonic device and will leave remembering what you taught!

NOTES

Preface

1. Kenneth Berding, *What Are Spiritual Gifts? Rethinking the Conventional View* (Grand Rapids, MI: Kregel, 2006).

Chapter 1: Walk in the Spirit

1. David S. Boyer, "Jerusalem to Rome in the Path of St. Paul," *The National Geographic Magazine* 150:6 (December, 1956): 710.

2. Unfortunately, some of our translations such as the NIV and the NLT almost always eliminate the *walk* metaphor and translate using the bland verb *live*. I believe that doing so loses something vital about the Christian life. Notice how many times the Greek word often translated "walk" (*peripateō*) is found as a summary in Paul's letters for living life (note: Gal. 5:25 uses a different Greek word): Romans 6:4; 8:4; 13:13; 14:15; 1 Corinthians 3:3; 7:17; 2 Corinthians 4:2; 5:7; 10:2; 10:3; 12:18; Galatians 5:16; Ephesians 2:2; 2:10; 4:1; 4:17; 5:2; 5:8; 5:15; Philippians 3:17; 3:18; Colossians 1:10; 2:6; 3:7; 4:5; 1 Thessalonians 2:12; 4:1; 4:12; 2 Thessalonians 3:6; 3:11.

Chapter 2: Set Your Mind on the Things of the Spirit

1. Leon Morris, *The Epistle to the Romans* (Grand Rapids: Eerdmans and Leicester: Inter-Varsity Press, 1988), 305.

2. Morris, *Romans*, 306.

3. Based on Helen H. Lemmel's "Turn Your Eyes upon Jesus," 1922.

Chapter 3: Put to Death the Deeds of the Body by the Spirit

1. "Trust and Obey," John H. Sammis, 1887.

Chapter 5: Know the Fatherhood of God by the Spirit

1. Joachim Jeremias, *The Prayers of Jesus* (London: SCM, 1967), 57ff, cited and supported in John R. W. Stott, *The Message of Romans: God's Good News for the World* (Leicester and Downers Grove: Inter-Varsity Press, 1994), 233.

2. David Crump, *Knocking on Heaven's Door: A New Testament Theology of Petitionary Prayer* (Grand Rapids: Baker Academic, 2006), 98n7.

3. Sirach 23:1; 51:10; 4Q372 1.16; Joseph and Aseneth 12:14–15. Cited in Crump, *Knocking on Heaven's Door*, 102.

Chapter 6: Hope in the Spirit

1. C. S. Lewis, *Mere Christianity* (New York: MacMillan, 1960), 118.

Chapter 7: Pray in the Spirit

1. Augustine, *Against the Manichees*, 1.22.34. Cited in Gerald Bray, ed. *Romans,* Ancient Christian Commentary on Scripture, gen. ed. Thomas C. Oden (Downers Grove, IL: InterVarsity Press, 1998), 222.

2. The first part of verse 27 has traditionally been understood to mean that God the Father, who searches human hearts, knows what the Holy Spirit is thinking. But this is probably not the correct way to read this Greek clause for a number of reasons (most not listed here), including parallels with similar expressions in Romans 8:5–7 and 1 Corinthians 2:10. I would argue (and have argued in a forthcoming journal article) that "the one who searches hearts" is the same main actor of the previous verse—the Holy Spirit—and that what the Spirit "knows" is that a believer has a mind-set that is focused on the Spirit. Kenneth Berding, "Who Searches Hearts and What Does He Know in Romans 8:27?," Evangelical Theological Society Annual Meeting, Atlanta, November 2010.

3. Quoted in Louis Gifford Parkhurst Jr., *The Believer's Secret of Intercession: Compiled from the Writings of Andrew Murray and C. H. Spurgeon* (Milton Keynes, England: Word Ltd., 1988), 63.

Appendix 1: Three Undercurrents in Romans 8

1. Everett F. Harrison, "Romans," in *Zondervan NIV Bible Commentary,* vol. 2: New Testament (Grand Rapids: Zondervan, 1994), 559.

SCRIPTURE INDEX